Memoirs of a Home Cook

Every Great Recipe Has a Story

By

Amy D. Currie

Amy –
Thanks for the inspiration!
XO, Amy

ISBN: 1-4140-1899-1 (e-book)
ISBN: 1-4140-1897-5 (Paperback)
ISBN: 1-4140-1898-3 (Dust Jacket)

Library of Congress Control Number: 2003097975

This book is printed on acid free paper.

Printed in the United States of America
Bloomington, IN

1stBooks - rev. 11/25/03

Acknowledgements

For Jimmy, Catie and William
and my
husband

Thank you Brooke, Christina, Betsy, Michael,
Alison, Jim and Mom

Contents

Forward

I've been cooking as long as I can remember. When I was 9, I saw the world through a glorious shade of purple. When I made my first batch of cookies they were, you guessed it, purple. Ingredients? I could have cared less. My beautiful, rock hard creations were mine all mine to share or to keep. It was at that moment that I began to understand the allure of the home cook. Of course, at the time I didn't really know how empowering home cooking could be, but I was aware that I could make friends out of enemies as long as I shared. In this case, my younger brothers, JB and Tom, would follow me around the house, stalking me like a celebrity all for one little cookie. After smelling that fresh baked smell and witnessing the chaos in the kitchen, they were bound and determined to get in on the cookie action.

Who doesn't like homemade? My grandmother, Nanny, was my inspiration. I spent plenty of time in Nanny's kitchen at her little table watching her create magic. She rarely measured, knew her recipes by heart, and was never short on advice. Quite simply, she was a natural at being the chief cook and matriarch of our family.

So, now it's my turn. Nothing is more inspiring than knowing I made a great, satisfying meal, whether it's a dinner party or a family celebration. But, the single greatest joy of cooking is simply cooking for my family everyday. When my kids ask me why their dinner tastes so good, I always have the same simple reply: It's made with love. It sounds too sentimental, but I see cooking as an ongoing memento that I give my children. The experience of watching, learning, helping, tasting and eating forms their memories and mine forever. This is so wonderful because they'll pass these cherished times as well as recipes to their children and so on and so on.

So here it is, my memoir in a neat little bundle. It's the best of my repertory and all the little stories that make a recipe so special. And they come from more places than you can imagine: old recipe boxes left in the attic, overheard conversations at the supermarket and innocent suggestions from my children, to name a few. But it's not just about the character of the recipe and the people who are gracious enough to share their cooking secrets. It's ultimately about taste and convenience combined with the pleasure of home cooking. So go ahead, read, cook, eat, share, enjoy!

Appetizers - Hors D'oeuvres

Unbelievable Cheese Crisps

Sometimes it seems like finding a good recipe is like a never-ending scavenger hunt. Like any creative process, the sky's the limit, so I'm constantly searching, tasting and appreciating wherever I go. Most people head for the bar when they walk into a party. I head for the hors d'oeuvres. I just have to taste everything, and then I can relax and enjoy myself. I know that sounds a little obsessive, but it's worth it because when I taste a "keeper" I can feel those creative cooking juices flowing. After tasting these unbelievable cheese crisps, I felt like I'd hit the jackpot. I suspected they had Rice Krispies in them, but doubted such an unusual ingredient. My friend, Lynne was gracious enough to share her recipe and sure enough, the secret ingredient was Rice Krispies. Wow! That's a keeper.

2 cups flour
2 t sugar
1/2 t salt
1/8 t cayenne pepper
1/8 t dry mustard
1 cup (2 sticks) unsalted butter, melted

dash Worcestershire sauce
4 cups (16 oz) sharp Cheddar cheese, grated
2 cups fresh Rice Krispies

- Preheat oven to 350°
- In a large bowl combine flour, sugar, salt, cayenne and mustard. Stir in butter and Worcestershire with a wooden spoon. Add cheese and stir to combine. Fold in Rice Krispies and very gently stir to combine
- Drop heaping teaspoons of dough on parchment lined baking sheets
- Bake 10-12 minutes until golden brown
- Cool on wire racks

Makes approximately 10 dozen

Gruyere Cheese Puffs (Gougeres)

This is a very versatile, easy recipe and I make them all the time for many purposes. Originally a French hors d'oeuvres, they're amazing right out of the oven, almost like a popover. But, don't limit these light and steamy puffs to hors d'oeuvres. Use them for brunch or at a dinner party instead of bread. Even your kids will adore them. You can add some fresh herbs or spices like thyme or cumin or place a dollop of chutney in the center. You can even slice them in half lengthwise and add a little ham to make mini sandwich hors d'oeuvres. It's fine to make them in advance and freeze although they loose a bit of freshness. Just re-heat 10 minutes before serving and you'll hardly know they weren't freshly baked.

1/2 cup (1 stick) unsalted butter
1 cup flour
1 cup whole milk
3/4 t salt
1/4 t pepper
1 T Dijon mustard
4 large eggs
1 cup (4 oz) Gruyere cheese, grated

- Preheat oven to 400°
- In a medium saucepan over medium heat, melt butter and heat milk. Remove from heat and sift in flour, salt and pepper stirring with a wooden spoon. Return to heat and stir vigorously until mixture forms a smooth ball. Continue stirring until a film forms over bottom of the pan, about 2 minutes
- Remove from heat and let cool 5 minutes. Whisk in mustard then eggs, one at a time and then cheese (cheese does not have to melt)
- Place dough in a pastry bag or a zip-top plastic bag with a cut off corner. Pipe tablespoons of dough 2" apart onto parchment lined baking sheets
- Bake 20 minutes until puffed and golden brown. Sprinkle with coarse salt while still warm

Makes approximately 40

Double Cheese Buttons

This was one of the first hors d'oeuvres I ever made and it seems like I've made them a million times. They're so good, I can't have them in the house or I'll eat every last one. If I had better will power, I'd keep a batch in the refrigerator ready to serve to drop-in guests. The combination of the Cheddar and blue cheeses gives them a unique, tangy flavor. The sesame seeds add a mellow nuttiness. They freeze well cooked, but should be frozen as dough. Then, you only cook as many as you need.

3/4 cup (1 1/2 sticks) unsalted butter, softened
2/3 cup (2 3/4 oz) Cheddar cheese, grated
2/3 cup (2 3/4 oz) blue cheese, crumbled
2 cups flour
2 t fresh chives, minced

1 t flat leaf parsley, chopped
1/2 t Worcestershire sauce
1/4 t cayenne pepper
1/8 t garlic powder
1 cup toasted sesame seeds

- In a large bowl, with an electric mixer, combine butter and cheeses until smooth. Add flour, chives, parsley, Worcestershire, cayenne and garlic powder until just combined
- Shape dough into a disc, wrap in plastic and chill 2 hours
- Preheat oven to 350°
- Roll tablespoons of dough into balls, then roll in sesame seeds
- Place on parchment lined baking sheets, 3" apart and flatten with a fork making a crisscross pattern
- Bake 12-14 minutes until edges are golden brown
- Cool on wire racks

Makes approximately 7 dozen

Cheddar Pecan Crisps

There is an art to entertaining. I like to compare it to a perfectly choreographed dance. If you are prepared and well organized, your guests will think you are a master at throwing a party. While a lot of work, if you stretch it out, you'll find yourself enjoying the whole process, not to mention the satisfaction of entertaining friends. These crisps look impressive on a bar or as a little extra to your menu. They can be made ahead of time and frozen. Here's a hint: when using nuts, toast them in a 350° oven for 8-10 minutes just until fragrant. This brings out the true flavor and really does make a difference in the recipe, especially this one.

1/2 cup (1 stick) unsalted butter, softened
2 cups (8 oz) Cheddar cheese, grated
1 large egg yolk
1/2 t salt
1/2 t cayenne pepper
2/3 cup flour
2/3 cup chopped pecans, toasted

- Preheat oven to 350°
- In a large bowl with an electric mixer, beat butter and cheese until smooth. Add egg yolk, and beat until combined. Sift in salt, cayenne, and flour until just combined. Gently fold in pecans
- Roll tablespoons of dough into balls and place on a parchment lined baking sheets, 3" apart. Flatten each ball with the bottom of a glass
- Bake 15-18 minutes until golden brown
- Cool on wire racks

Makes approximately 4 dozen

Sesame Wonton Crisps

There is nothing worse than having a delicious dip on a terrible cracker. So much time is spent making the dip, which gets all the attention while the cracker or chip resembles a piece of cardboard. Sure, there are many perfectly tasty store bought crackers, but these crisps are quick to make, healthy because they're baked and tasty all by themselves. More importantly, they'll showcase your dip like no cracker can.

2 T canola oil
4 t cornstarch
12 oz package wonton wrappers (approximately 50)
4 T toasted sesame seeds
2 T coarse salt

- Preheat oven to 375°
- In a small bowl, whisk together oil and cornstarch
- Stack 17 wonton wrappers and cut in half diagonally. Arrange in one layer on a large baking sheet. Repeat 2 more times
- Brush tops with oil mixture. Sprinkle with sesame seeds and salt
- Bake 5-6 minutes until golden brown

Makes approximately 8 dozen

Clam and Scallion Wontons

My friends, Becky, Christina and I regularly get our kids together on Fridays, kind of like a kiddy happy hour. Between the three of us, we have nine, all under the age of eight. You can imagine the bedlam between the hours of 4-6 every Friday evening! We have two rules that keep us sane: 1) if necessary, yelling at children other than your own is perfectly fine 2) plenty of wine and hors d'oeuvres for us. Play group is my time to experiment because I know my friends will be as brutally honest as only good friends can be. In the case of this hors d'oeuvre, though, it was the kids who approved wholeheartedly. When they thought we weren't looking, they did the old grab and run. Lucky for them, rule #1 did not apply.

12 oz package wonton wrappers
2, 8 oz packages cream cheese, softened
3 scallions, trimmed and sliced
1/2 t soy sauce + more for dipping
3 drops sesame oil
1 t fresh ginger, grated
2, 6.5 oz cans chopped clams, drained
2 T unsalted butter, melted

- Preheat oven 425°
- In a medium bowl with a wooden spoon, mix cream cheese, scallions, soy sauce, sesame oil, ginger, and clams
- Place 1 teaspoon of the mixture in the center of each wonton wrapper. Fold in half to form a triangle. Wet edge to seal
- Place triangles on parchment lined baking sheets and brush with melted butter.
- Bake 12 minutes until golden brown
- Serve with soy sauce for dipping

Makes 3-4 dozen

Bacon Toasties

This is my friend Christina's recipe and we all call it the "king" of hors d'oeuvres. They taste amazing and I have never known anyone not to like them young or old. My kids beg for them and it's always the first thing to go at a party. I keep the ingredients handy and when I make bacon on the weekends, I make a little extra for the toasties. Since they have to be frozen, I always have a supply ready to go.

2 cups (8 oz) white sharp Cheddar cheese, grated
1/2 cup mayonnaise
1 cup sliced almonds, toasted
1 small onion, chopped
1 t Worcestershire sauce
8-10 strips bacon cooked, drained and crumbled
16 oz package cocktail party rye or sourdough, crusts removed

- In a large bowl with a wooden spoon mix all ingredients. Spread 1 heaping tablespoon on each piece of bread. Mold to cover entire piece of bread. Freeze 2 hours to overnight in zip-top bags
- Preheat oven to 400°
- Cut frozen toasties diagonally into triangles. Place on parchment lined baking sheets. Bake 10-12 minutes until bubbly

Makes approximately 5 dozen

Sausage Toasties

If bacon toasties are the "king" of hors d'oeuvres, sausage toasties are the "queen" They're so easy to make and so utterly indulgent, it's always a party when they're served. Since they have to be frozen, you just pop them in the oven when your company arrives, even if your company is you and your significant other after a long day.

1 lb bulk breakfast sausage
2 cups (8 oz) sharp Cheddar cheese, grated
1 t Worcestershire sauce
1 t dried oregano
1 t garlic powder
16 oz package cocktail party rye, crusts removed

- In a large skillet, brown sausage, then drain grease. Return cooked sausage to skillet over low heat. Add cheese and stir until melted. Stir in Worcestershire, oregano and garlic powder
- Spread 1 heaping tablespoon on each piece of bread. Mold to cover entire piece of bread. Freeze 2 hours to overnight in zip-top bags
- Preheat oven to 400°
- Cut frozen toasties into triangles. Place on parchment lined baking sheets. Bake 10-12 minutes until bubbly.

Makes approximately 5 dozen

Sausage Cheese Balls

When it comes to celebrating religious holidays, we are one busy family. I was raised Jewish and my husband, Jim was raised Catholic. Because of this, we embrace most of the holidays. Our kids get to celebrate "everything". We create new traditions with each holiday that only enrich both of our religions. When it comes to Christmas, I've jumped in with both feet. Every year, we have an open house on Christmas day with our extended families. The fireplace is roaring and the kids are blissfully insane and we feast from lunch straight through dinner. Sausage cheese balls are a traditional favorite at our open house and a perfect addition to any holiday menu.

1 lb bulk breakfast sausage
2/3 cup flour
2 cups (8 oz) sharp Cheddar cheese, grated
1 small onion, chopped
1 celery stalk, chopped
1/4 t garlic powder

- Pre-heat oven to 375°
- In a large bowl, mix all ingredients and form into 1 1/2" balls. Place on a rimmed baking sheet lined with non-stick aluminum foil
- Bake 25-30 minutes until golden brown (can be frozen prior to serving, cooked or uncooked)

Makes approximately 3 dozen

Asparagus Canapés

My kids love white bread and they beg me to buy it. But, to their profound disappointment, wheat bread is healthier. The problem is, the spongy white stuff make great hors d'oeuvres. When I buy it for asparagus canapés, I have to hide it. If I could use some other type of bread, I would, but it would compromise the recipe. White bread Makes these hors d'oeuvres crunchy, chewy and delicious. So, the closest my kids will ever get to fulfill their wish is having an asparagus canapé. But, they refuse to eat asparagus, so I guess white bread is just not in their future.

8 oz package cream cheese, softened
1 cup (4 oz) blue cheese, crumbled
1 T mayonnaise
1 large egg
18 slices white bread, crusts removed
18 asparagus spears, trimmed and blanched
5 T unsalted butter, melted

- In a food processor combine cheeses, mayonnaise, and egg until smooth. Chill 1 hour
- Preheat oven to 400°
- With a rolling pin, flatten bread. Spread each slice with 2 tablespoons cheese mixture. Place 1 asparagus spear on bread. Roll up and slice in half on a diagonal. Place on a baking sheet lined with parchment paper
- Brush with melted butter and bake 15 minutes until golden brown (can be frozen uncooked)

Makes 3 dozen

Dill Marinated Broccoli with Lemon Curry Dip

The crudités platter is a fixture for every type of entertaining from casual barbecue to elegant dinner party. What could be better than brightly colored, beautifully arranged fresh and healthy vegetables especially if it's enhanced with a delicious dip? Here's a twist on this favorite. My mother-in-law, Dottie, discovered this tasty way to serve broccoli with an equally tasty dip. She told me the guests couldn't get enough of it and I am so glad she was persistent in getting the recipe because now I can enjoy it!

2 lbs broccoli (about 2 bunches) trimmed into florets
3/4 cup canola oil
1/4 cup apple cider vinegar
2 t sugar
1 bunch fresh dill, trimmed and finely chopped
5-6 garlic cloves, peeled and cut in half

Dip
1 cup mayonnaise
juice and zest of 1 lemon
1 t curry powder

- In a zip-top bag combine oil, vinegar, sugar, dill and garlic. Add broccoli then seal and shake
- Refrigerate overnight occasionally shaking
- Drain broccoli and remove garlic. Place broccoli on serving platter with toothpicks.
- Dip: Combine mayonnaise, lemon juice, zest and curry powder in a small bowl

Serves 8-10

Zucchini Pancakes with Chive Crème Fraiche

One summer, we were visiting my Dad at the beach when someone gave him a giant zucchini from his garden, which was the size of a small watermelon. It sat on the kitchen table all weekend lonely and neglected. Pre-occupied with barbecuing and trips to the ice cream parlor, no one knew what to do with this mammoth vegetable. I decided to turn it into dozens of tiny little zucchini pancakes. To my surprise, every pancake was eaten. I used this gigantic zucchini out of desperation, but I don't recommend cooking with one this size. The seeds are too big and not that attractive or tasty. The smaller zucchinis are more delicate in taste and texture. The pancakes can also be cooked then frozen. Prior to serving, just warm them in the oven, then top with the chive crème fraiche.

Pancakes
4 cups (about 1 lb) zucchini, finely grated
1/4 cup flour
1/4 cup (1 oz) Parmesan cheese, freshly grated
2 t flat leaf parsley, chopped

2 large egg whites
4 T canola oil
Chive Crème Fraiche
1 cup crème fraiche or sour cream
2 T fresh chives, chopped

- Place zucchini in a colander and let sit for 20 minutes to drain, then wrap in a kitchen towel and twist to drain out as much liquid as possible. Transfer to a medium bowl and toss with flour, Parmesan, and parsley
- In a large bowl, beat egg whites until foamy. Gently fold in zucchini mixture
- Heat 1 tablespoon oil in a large skillet over medium/high heat. Drop 1 tablespoon of batter at a time to make mini pancakes. Fill the skillet with as many pancakes as possible cooking about 1 minute on each side. Transfer to paper towels to drain and cool. Repeat until batter is finished
- Meanwhile mix crème fraiche and chives in a small bowl

- Place pancakes on a serving platter with a dollop of crème fraiche. Sprinkle additional chives on top

Makes approximately 2 dozen

Tomato Tart

I don't know how it happened or how it began. I became rather well known for my tomato tart. It's not a very original recipe. I actually see it in print all the time. It's never exactly like mine and the name is always different, but the basic idea is there. It can be served any time of day: brunch, lunch, dinner, or hors d'oeuvres. With only four ingredients in the filling, it's ridiculously easy to make. Couldn't I be known for something more complicated or better yet, more sophisticated? I guess at the end of the day, it really is pretty close to a perfect recipe, so I think I'll embrace my notoriety.

Crust
1 1/4 cups flour
1/2 t salt
1/2 cup (1 stick) unsalted butter,
chilled and cut into small pieces
3-4 T ice cold water
        or
1 refrigerated pie crust

Filling:
2 T Dijon mustard
1 cup (4 oz) Gruyere
cheese, grated
1 large tomato, thinly sliced
2 T fresh basil, chopped

- Crust: Place flour and salt in a food processor and process for a few seconds to combine. Add butter and process until mixture looks like coarse crumbs. Add ice water in a slow, steady stream until dough holds together
- Turn onto floured work surface and form a disc. Wrap in plastic and chill 30 minutes
- Preheat oven to 350°
- Filling: Place dough in a 9" removable bottom tart pan. Crimp to make an edge around pan and prick a few holes with a fork on bottom
- Bake 20 minutes until slightly brown
- Spread mustard on bottom, then cheese in an even layer. Arrange tomato slices over cheese and bake 30 minutes until tomatoes begin to look dry. Sprinkle with basil, salt, and pepper to taste.

Serves 6-8

Caramelized Onion Tart

Of all of the vegetables out there, nothing is more versatile than the onion. Onions can be found in almost every savory dish and this diversity gives them their split personality. Their strong odor and harshness assaults you, making your eyes water. When you start cooking them, they mellow out and the longer you cook them, the sweeter and sweeter they get. This caramelized onion tart takes the flavor to the max. After about an hour of cooking over low heat, they become so soft and sticky your mouth will water just looking at the pan. Your home will be filled with the undeniable smell of the buttery rich caramelized vegetable.

Crust:
1 1/4 cups flour
1/2 t salt
1/2 cup (1 stick) unsalted butter,
chilled and cut into small pieces
3-4 T ice cold water or
1 refrigerated pie crust
Filling:
2 T butter

2 T olive oil
3 Spanish or Vidalia onions
thinly sliced
2 shallots, thinly sliced
2 sprigs fresh thyme
1 T sherry vinegar
3/4 cup heavy cream
2 large egg yolks

- Crust: Place flour and salt in a food processor and process for a few seconds to combine. Add butter and process until mixture looks like coarse crumbs. Add ice water in a slow, steady stream until dough holds together
- Turn onto a floured work surface and form into a disc. Wrap in plastic and chill 30 minutes
- Filling: In a large skillet over medium/low heat, sauté onions, shallots, and thyme in butter and oil. Season with salt and pepper. Stir occasionally until onions are soft and caramelized, about 1 hour (add a splash of water if mixture seems dry). Remove thyme branches and stir in vinegar. Set aside
- Preheat oven to 350°

- Place dough in a 9" removable bottom tart pan. Crimp to make an edge around pan and prick a few holes with a fork on bottom. Bake 10 minutes until lightly brown
- In a bowl whisk together heavy cream and egg yolks. Add to onion mixture. Pour onion mixture into crust and bake until set, 30 minutes.

Serves 8-10

Prosciutto and Gruyere Pinwheels

If I had to limit the contents of my refrigerator to 10 items, one of them would definitely be puff pastry. It is incredibly versatile and it goes both ways; sweet or savory. This particular hors d'oeuvre is so easy it's ridiculous. First of all, you only need 4 ingredients (assuming your puff pastry is one of the ten ingredients in your freezer). Second, after it's made, you throw it back in the refrigerator or freezer until you need it. If you wrap it tightly, it can stay in there for several weeks. Oh, and by the way, you can get your kids involved in the process up to the rolling part. They'll enjoy doing this because they'll absolutely love eating the finished product. Now, here's the tricky part: when slicing the chilled logs, use a serrated knife and slowly saw through the dough to keep the slice intact. If it is not a perfectly formed pinwheel before it goes into the oven, it will come apart and look like a broken rainbow. If this happens, just say your kids made that one.

1 sheet puff pastry (half of a 17.3 oz package)
4 oz prosciutto, thinly sliced
2 T basil, chopped
3/4 cup (3 oz) Gruyere cheese, grated
1 large egg, beaten

- Place pastry sheet on a work surface. Cut in half forming two 9 1/2 x 5" rectangles. Arrange half the prosciutto on 1 rectangle leaving a 1/2" border along the long side. Sprinkle with half the basil and then half the cheese. Brush plain 1/2" border with egg
- Starting at the long side opposite the border, roll-up jelly roll style, pressing to seal the long edge. Wrap in plastic. Repeat with remaining ingredients. Chill 2 hours
- Preheat oven to 400°
- Cut logs into 1/2" thick slices. Place on parchment lined baking sheets and bake 15 minutes until golden brown
- Cool on wire racks

Makes approximately 2 1/2 dozen

19

Mozzarella Stuffed Mushrooms

When I think of stuffed mushrooms, I am reminded of the hors d'oeuvres I used to pass out at my parents cocktail parties when I was a kid. The thrill of staying up late and feeling like a grown up was so exciting even if I was wearing my pajamas. The stuffed mushrooms that I passed around seemed so elegant. The earthy and herby aroma so heady. I tried to recreate that memory and it has not lost its charm.

24 large mushrooms, cleaned
4 T (1/2 stick) unsalted butter
2 shallots, minced
1 leek, trimmed and chopped
3 garlic cloves, minced
1 T fresh thyme, chopped
1 cup bread crumbs (panko*)

3 T heavy cream
2 large egg yolks
1/2 cup (2 oz) mozzarella cheese, grated
1/2 cup (2 oz) Parmesan cheese, freshly grated

- Preheat oven to 375°
- Remove mushroom stems and finely chop. Set aside
- Arrange mushrooms caps rounded side down in a 13x9" baking dish
- In a medium skillet over medium/high heat sauté mushroom stems, shallots, leeks, garlic and thyme in butter until soft, 5 minutes. Add bread crumbs and stir 5 more minutes. Season with salt and pepper. Turn off heat. Whisk heavy cream and egg yolks. Mix into stuffing
- Sprinkle mozzarella evenly in mushroom caps, then stuffing. Top with Parmesan
- Bake 20 minutes until bubbly

Makes 2 dozen

---

* Japanese breadcrumbs

20

Mushroom, Prosciutto and Gorgonzola Crostini

Last spring, a friend asked me to make her some hors d'oeuvres and insisted on having crostini. I'd never worked with toasted baguette slices, but how hard could it be? I was more interested in topping the bread and I prepared an amazing combination of mushroom, prosciutto and blue cheese. I carefully sliced and toasted the fresh baguette. Well, the bread slices turned to charcoal in like two seconds flat. So, I bought another baguette and did it again! At this point, the party was starting in 1/2 hour and the bakery was closed. I went to the pasta restaurant in town and begged for a loaf of bread. Finally it turned out just right. The moral of the story: watch your crostini when you toast it and get to know your local Italian restaurant!

3 T unsalted butter
2, 10 oz packages mushrooms,
stems removed and chopped
2 garlic cloves, minced
1/2 cup heavy cream
1/2 cup (2 oz) Gorgonzola
cheese, crumbled

1/2 cup (2 1/2 oz) chopped
prosciutto
1 long thin baguette in 1/2"
slices
chopped flat leaf parsley
for garnish

- Preheat oven to 375°
- In a large skillet over medium heat, sauté mushrooms and garlic in butter until mushrooms release their liquid, 8 minutes. Add cream and cook until liquid is completely absorbed, 2 minutes. Turn off heat. Add Gorgonzola and prosciutto and stir until cheese melts. Season with salt and pepper to taste. Set aside
- Toast bread slices 5 minutes until golden. Mound 1 tablespoon of topping on each crostini. Return to oven 5 more minutes to heat through. Sprinkle with chopped parsley

Makes approximately 2 dozen

Pâté and Green Tomato Jam Crostini

When Jim and I first started dating, we quickly learned how much we both loved and appreciated fine food like smoked salmon, cheese, caviar and pâté. Looking back, it's hard to believe that sometimes we'd have a simple yet elegant dinner of just that with a bottle of wine. Living in New York, we had no trouble finding all sorts of delicious vittles. These days, being a bit older and more health conscious, we'll have one delicacy at a time and on that occasion when we're feeling a little indulgent, this is one of the hors d'oeuvres I like to make. The sweet and sour green tomato jam acts as a great compliment to the pâté. So, enjoy this with your special someone, raise a glass of wine, and toast the moment.

2 green tomatoes, seeded and chopped
3/4 cup sugar
zest from 1 lemon
8 oz (1/2 lb) truffle mousse pâté
1 long thin baguette in 1/2" slices

- In a saucepan over medium/high heat, cook tomatoes, lemon zest and sugar for 15 minutes. Remove from heat cover and chill, 3 hours
- Preheat oven to 375°
- Toast bread slices 5 minutes until golden. Spread a thin layer of pâté on bread and top with a 1/2 teaspoon of jam or more to taste (if you prefer, substitute pâté with sharp Cheddar cheese)

Makes approximately 2 dozen

Firecracker Shrimp

When it comes to New Years Eve, there is a good chance you'll find Jim and me at home. It's not that we don't like to celebrate the end of one year and the beginning of another, we just love to do it at home. We weren't always like this, but since we've had children, we like ringing in the New Year with our family all together. We begin our evening with cocktails and hors d'oeuvres. The kids have sparkling cider, we have champagne and we all have firecracker shrimp. We tell the kids that these are their fireworks since they are not quite old enough to make it to midnight to see the real thing. Then, we have a big family toast and off they go to bed. What could be better than that?

12 jumbo shrimp (about 1 lb), shelled with tail on
3 T olive oil
juice and zest from 1 lemon
1/4 t cayenne pepper
2 t fresh thyme, chopped
2 T flat leaf parsley, chopped
6 slices prosciutto (2 oz), sliced in half lengthwise to make 12 slices

- In a zip-top bag, combine oil, lemon zest, cayenne, thyme and parsley. Add shrimp and toss to coat. Chill 1 hour
- Remove shrimp and discard marinade. Wrap each shrimp with one slice of prosciutto
- Heat grill on high. Grill shrimp 2 minutes on each side until prosciutto has charcoal marks (Can also be broiled in the oven)

Makes 1 dozen

Smoked Salmon Pinwheels

Our friends Ann and Rick recently returned from living in Europe for several years. So, when we were at their house for cocktails, Ann served this sophisticated smoked salmon pinwheel hors d'oeuvre that she picked up while on her travels abroad. It looked impossibly complicated to make, yet Ann assured me it could not be easier. I love this recipe because my friends' experiences abroad have broadened my own knowledge of how food is enjoyed in other parts of the World.

12 oz package sliced, smoked salmon
8 oz package cream cheese, softened
1 t lemon zest
1 t fresh dill, chopped
1/2 t salt

2 cucumbers, sliced
or
16 oz package party pumpernickel bread

- Place a sheet of plastic wrap 24 x12" on a work surface. Arrange salmon slices on plastic wrap in a 20 x 12" rectangle, leaving 2" edge of plastic wrap on each end
- In a medium bowl with an electric mixer, beat cream cheese, lemon zest, dill and salt until smooth. Spread in an even layer over salmon. With the long end, roll jelly-roll style. Wrap salmon with the plastic wrap. Freeze 2 hours
- With a sharp, serrated knife, cut into 36 1/2" slices
- Serve on cucumber rounds or party pumpernickel bread

Makes approximately 3 dozen

Deviled Eggs

Years ago when I worked in advertising in New York City, I would meet my sister-in-law at a famous, fabulously trendy department store for lunch. We always got the same thing, fresh pea soup and deviled eggs. The deviled eggs were Christy's idea. She loved them and could polish off a whole plate before I could even finish a story. I grew to love them too, but mostly because of the allure of being invisible for a quick hour before facing the reality of work again. This one's for you, Christy.

1 dozen large eggs
1/4 cup mayonnaise
1/4 cup Dijon mustard
4 T (1/2 stick) unsalted butter, softened
1 t fresh lemon juice
1/4 t cayenne pepper
chopped chives for garnish

- Place eggs in a pan large enough to hold them in a single layer. Cover with cold water by 1 inch. Bring to a boil, cover and turn off heat. Let stand 15 minutes. Drain under cold water until eggs are cool
- Peel, cut in half, remove yolks and place yolks in a bowl. Add mayonnaise, mustard and butter and mix until smooth. Stir in lemon juice, cayenne, salt and pepper to taste
- Place in a pastry bag or a zip-top plastic bag with a cut off corner. Pipe into egg whites. Garnish with chives

Makes 24

Baked Brie with Raspberries

Baked Brie means celebration in our family, and if I don't make it at every holiday gathering, I'm in big trouble. The flaky pastry, the tart raspberries, and the gooey, melted Brie are irresistible and make a spectacular presentation. You can do the sauce ahead of time and refrigerate until you are ready to use. The large wheel of Brie is easier to find around the holidays in December. If you can't find it, ask your grocery store to order it for you.

6 oz container fresh raspberries
1/2 cup packed light brown sugar + 1T
1/2 cup raisins
4 T (1/2 cup) unsalted butter
1 T soy sauce
1 t fresh lemon juice
1/2 cup sliced almonds, toasted
2.2 lb (1 kilo) wheel of Brie cheese
1 sheet of puff pastry (half of a 17.3 oz package)
1 large egg yolk

- In a small saucepan over medium/high heat combine raspberries, 1/2 cup brown sugar, raisins, butter, soy sauce and lemon juice. Bring to a boil; reduce heat to low and cook covered until raspberries are no longer whole, 5 minutes. Turn off heat and cool to room temperature
- Preheat oven to 325°
- Place Brie on an oven proof platter. With a fork, prick a few holes in top. Spoon half of the raspberry mixture on top (freeze the rest for another time). Sprinkle almonds over top. Place puff pastry on top of Brie tucking the edges under. Whisk egg yolk with 1 tablespoon water. Brush over Brie. Sprinkle 1 tablespoon brown sugar on top
- Bake 30 minutes until puffed and golden
- Let rest 15 minutes before serving

Serves 20-25

Appetizers - Dips and Spreads

Fresh Spinach Dip

In the world of entertaining, if hors d'oeuvres are royalty, dips are the common folk. They just don't have a great image. First of all, the name dip brings it down from the beginning. Yes, it's a practical name, but who wants to spend time at a party standing around a bowl dipping. Then there's double dipping, which could really ruin one's appetite. There are ways around this dilemma, as many dips are better presented as an individual hors d'oeuvre. Take this spinach dip, for example. The color and texture of the fresh spinach makes a beautiful presentation on a Belgian endive leaf or a slice of toasted baguette.

2 T olive oil
1 small onion, chopped
1 shallot, chopped
5 oz bag of baby spinach
4 oz cream cheese, softened
8 oz container of sour cream

- In a medium skillet over medium heat, sauté onion and shallot in oil until lightly browned, about 10 minutes. Add spinach and toss until wilted, 1 minute. Transfer spinach, cream cheese and sour cream to a food processor and pulse to combine. Season with salt and pepper to taste
- Cover and chill 1 hour

Makes approximately 2 cups

Portobello Mushroom Spread

Visiting other cities and having different unique culinary experiences is my idea of fun. Every summer, we visit Jim's parents in Chicago and I always look forward to the local tastes of the region. Last time a little gourmet take-out store got me really excited. My mother-in-law, Dottie, sent me into the store to pick up their famous salsa while she waited in the car (I thought you didn't have to do this stuff after age 12). I walked in and discovered a refrigerator full of dips and spreads. There must have been twenty different types and I wanted to try them all. The Portobello dip was my favorite. Here's my version.

2 Portobello mushroom caps, chopped
2 shallots, chopped
2 T unsalted butter
2 T olive oil
3 scallions, trimmed and chopped
4 oz cream cheese, softened
8 oz container of sour cream
1 T soy sauce
1 T sherry
dash garlic powder

- In a large skillet, over medium heat sauté shallots in butter and oil until soft, 2 minutes. Add mushrooms and sauté until they release their liquid, 8 minutes
- Transfer mushrooms, scallions, cream cheese, sour cream, soy sauce, sherry and garlic powder to a food processor and pulse to combine
- Season with salt and pepper to taste
- Cover and chill 1 hour

Makes approximately 2 cups

Pico De Gallo Dip

I have a love hate relationship with salsa. If it's freshly made, the flavors are so clean and sharp; they seem to jump right off the tortilla chip. If it's a little older than that, it gets a watery consistency, which drives me crazy. Anything in a jar, well, forget it. This dip, a tasty alternative, is mellow and rich, and will hold its shape throughout your party. Even a chip can get through this dip.

1 medium tomato, seeded and coarsely chopped
1/2 cup fresh cilantro, chopped
1/2 small red onion, chopped
1 jalapeno, seeded and minced
4 oz cream cheese, softened
8 oz container sour cream

- Place all ingredients in a food processor and pulse to combine
- Season with salt and pepper to taste
- Cover and chill for 1 hour

Makes approximately 2 cups

Reuben Dip

I was one of about 50 women at a meeting last year to discuss a local fundraiser. There were several bowls of chips and candy scattered about as we stood around waiting for the meeting to begin. My friend Jennifer walked in holding a platter with steam trailing behind her. I heard the gasps before I smelled the dish. The ladies were shrieking. "She brought the Reuben dip", said one breathlessly, and it was gone in 5 minutes. It was surprisingly delicious, just like a Reuben sandwich. The Super Bowl was coming up and I knew Jim would love it, so she gave me the recipe and I've been making it ever since.

8 oz package of cream cheese, softened
1/2 cup Thousand Island salad dressing
4 oz (1/4 lb) deli corned beef (extra lean), chopped
1 1/2 (6 oz) cups Swiss cheese, grated
1/2 cup well drained sauerkraut

- Preheat oven to 350°
- In a medium bowl, with a wooden spoon, mix cream cheese, Thousand Island dressing, corned beef and 1 cup Swiss cheese. Pour in a 9" quiche pan or 8" square baking pan
- Spread sauerkraut on top followed by remaining cheese
- Bake 20 minutes until bubbly
- Serve hot with crackers

Serves 15- 20

Hot Pizza Dip

A few years ago, our neighbors Jon and Ceci had a party. It was the end of the summer and most people had just come back from vacation. It was a warm, beautiful night and because of the time of year, it started to get dark fairly early. Ceci lit beautiful handmade votives on every table, which gave their backyard a magical glow. Jim and I discovered a mysterious dip on one of the tables that was so good, we sat there silently devouring it. But, it was too dark to tell what it was. After almost eating the entire thing, I had to know, what in the world was it? Caroline, another neighbor, laughed at my desperation when she told me it was her specialty, hot pizza dip.

8 oz package of cream cheese, softened
1/2 cup sour cream
1 t dried oregano
1/8 t crushed red pepper
1/2 cup pizza sauce
1/2 cup pepperoni, chopped
3 scallions, trimmed and chopped
1/2 green pepper, seeded and chopped
2 oz (1/2 cup) mozzarella cheese, grated

- Preheat oven to 350°
- In small bowl, combine cream cheese, sour cream, oregano and red pepper. Spread in a 9" quiche pan or 8" square baking pan. Spread sauce over cheese mixture. Sprinkle with pepperoni, scallions and green pepper
- Bake 10 minutes
- Top with mozzarella and bake 10 more minutes until bubbly
- Serve hot with crackers

Serves 15-20

Hot Spinach-Parmesan Dip

When one's invited to a party, it's generally polite to enquire if you can bring anything. I'm always thrilled to help. Unless you're having your party catered, it can be a lot of work. Having guests contribute allows you to do a really good job on fewer dishes. The problem with bringing something is that it must be pre-cooked and needs to be sturdy enough to survive the trip to the party. Hot dips in particular are a challenge. I can't tell you how many potholders I've lost transporting a steaming hot, bubbling dish to a party. Should Jim make the slightest jerky movement while driving, our night could be over, not to mention our marriage. After too many burns on my thighs, I came up with a solution. I make my dip earlier in the day, place it in a container, then the refrigerator. I bring it to the party that way with a serving dish on the side. In five minutes it's in the oven and ten minutes after that it's ready to serve.

2 T unsalted butter
2 T olive oil
1 medium onion, chopped
2 garlic cloves, minced
1 T flour
1/2 cup chicken broth
1/2 cup heavy cream

10 oz package baby spinach
1 cup (4oz) Parmesan cheese, grated
1/4 cup sour cream
dash cayenne pepper
1 long, thin baguette, sliced

- Pre-heat oven to 350°
- In a large skillet over medium heat, sauté onion and garlic in butter and oil until soft, 5 minutes. Add flour and stir until absorbed, 1 minute. Add broth and cream and bring to a boil whisking constantly. Cook until mixture thickens, 2 minutes. Remove from heat. Add spinach and toss until wilted
- In a food processor pulse spinach mixture with 3/4 cup Parmesan, sour cream and cayenne until just combined
- Transfer to a 9" quiche pan or 8" square baking dish. Sprinkle with 1/4 cup Parmesan and bake 15 minutes until bubbly
- Serve warm with baguette slices

Serves 10-15

Hot Mushroom and Artichoke Spread

I have a lot of cooking idols and one cooking mentor. The idols are all inaccessible cookbook authors and TV personalities. My cooking mentor is Mrs. Macpherson. She's a cookbook author too. In fact, she has written three cookbooks and cultivated a successful catering business all while raising a family. She's very well known locally and her latest cookbook is the bible of entertaining. Everybody knows of her, but I'm lucky because I know her well. She's my friend Betsy's mother-in-law and I regularly see her on the soccer field or baseball diamond as she cheers on her grandchildren and I cheer on my kids. I'm always asking for advice and she graciously rewards me. Once, I was explaining how nervous I was cooking my first Thanksgiving dinner. She rattled off dozens of tips including no hors d'oeuvres on Thanksgiving. "But that's my favorite part", I mumbled. I struggled with this for days. I knew she was right, but in the end, it was my meal so I compromised and served only one.

1 t olive oil
10 oz package mushrooms, sliced
1/2 cup mayonnaise
1/4 cup (1 oz) Parmesan cheese, freshly grated
1/2 celery stalk, chopped
1/2 small onion, chopped
1 scallion, trimmed and chopped
2 T flat leaf parsley, chopped

1 t garlic powder
1/4 t cayenne pepper
14 oz can artichoke hearts, drained and chopped
2, 8 oz packages cream cheese, softened
1 long, thin baguette, sliced

- Preheat oven to 350°
- In a large skillet over medium heat, sauté mushrooms in oil until they release their liquid, 8 minutes. Roughly chop
- In a large bowl with a wooden spoon, combine mushrooms with remaining ingredients until well blended
- Transfer to a 9" quiche pan or 8" square baking dish. Bake 30 minutes until bubbly
- Serve warm with baguette slices

Serves 15- 20

Artichoke-Prosciutto Gratin

Every Friday afternoon, in preparation of our playgroup, my friends Becky and Christina and I make a trip to the local cheese shop for some goodies. It's always three different cheeses and one has to be stinky. Paul at the cheese shop knows us gals by that same order every Friday. Yes, we love stinky cheese like a good Muenster or blue. So, I had to laugh when a friend of mine asked me if I had any good artichoke recipes. I gave her this one. The following week, she told me it was a great success except her whole house stunk from it. Well, that was music to my ears and the sign of a great hors d'oeuvre. It's just a matter of whom you ask.

2, 14 oz cans artichoke hearts, drained and quartered
6 oz (1/3 lb) thinly sliced prosciutto
1 cup heavy cream
1 1/2 cups (6 oz) Gorgonzola cheese, crumbled
1/2 cup pine nuts, toasted
1/4 cup (1 oz) Parmesan cheese, freshly grated
1 T fresh sage, chopped
1 long, thin baguette, sliced

- Preheat oven to 350°
- Pat artichokes dry. Cut each prosciutto slice in half lengthwise and wrap each artichoke quarter. Place wrapped artichoke in a 9" quiche pan or 8" square baking dish. Pour cream over, then sprinkle gorgonzola, pine nuts, Parmesan and sage
- Bake 25 minutes until bubbly
- Serve warm with baguette slices

Serves 8-10

Chunky Clam Dip

I don't save hors d'oeuvres just for entertaining; I like to put out
something before regular family dinners too. But making one that
everyone likes can be challenging because of my picky tasters. For
them it's too spicy or smells funny or is just not geared towards kids.
This is one dip that everyone likes.

2, 6 1/2 oz cans chopped clams
6 slices bacon, cooked, drained and crumbled
8 oz package of cream cheese, softened
1/4 cup sour cream
1/2 red pepper, seeded and chopped
3 scallions, trimmed and chopped
1/4 cup (packed) basil, chopped
1 t fresh lemon juice
1 t drained, bottled horseradish
1/2 t Worcestershire sauce
dash hot sauce

- Drain clams and reserving 2 tablespoons juice
- In a medium bowl whisk together all ingredients including clam
  juice
- Cover and chill 1 hour.

Makes approximately 2 cups

White Bean and Rosemary Spread

I love this dip because it's so healthy and easy to make. But, over the years, I've adapted the cooking methodology to my daily routine. After the beans are soaked overnight, I bring all the ingredients to a boil while my kids are having breakfast. Just as it starts boiling, I turn off the heat and leave the beans in the pot, lid closed, while I take the kids to school and go to the gym. After the gym, I go to the bakery to get a fresh baguette. By lunchtime the beans are soft and cooled. I throw it all in the food processor, add the oil, toast the baguette and I have a delicious lunch. It's so unscientific, but it works every time.

8 oz (1/2 lb) dried navy beans
2, 14 oz cans chicken broth
2 garlic cloves, peeled
2 sprigs fresh rosemary
1/4 cup olive oil

- Place beans in a pot, cover with water and soak overnight
- Drain in a colander
- Place beans in a medium saucepan. Add chicken broth, garlic and rosemary. Bring to a boil, reduce to a simmer, cover and cook 1 1/2 hours until beans are soft. Remove from heat and cool to room temperature. Remove rosemary stems
- Transfer to a food processor and add oil until combined, but still a little chunky. Season with salt and pepper to taste
- Cover and chill 1 hour

Makes approximately 2 cups

Black Bean Hummus

One of the most important aspects of having a successful party is planning the perfect balance of hors d'oeuvres. This depth of planning goes in several different directions. First, you want to make sure there is something for everyone. Surprise! You've invited a vegetarian so make sure you have something for them to eat. It doesn't have to be the focus of your menu, but at the same time you want to be considerate. Second, keep it balanced. If you have a big platter of cheese and crackers, some puff pastry things and a bowl of chips and dip, your guests will not only be full before dinner, they may be feeling a bit sick too. I always round out my menu with a crudités or vegetable platter. Black bean hummus is perfect with this and, just in case, it's vegetarian too.

15 oz can black beans, rinsed and drained (reserving liquid)
2 T tahini (sesame paste)
juice of 1 lemon
1/4 cup (packed) cilantro
2 scallions, trimmed and sliced
1 T olive oil
1 t ground cumin
1/2 t cayenne pepper

- In a food processor, combine all ingredients until smooth (Add 1-2 tablespoons reserved bean liquid if needed). Season with salt and pepper to taste
- Cover and chill 1 hour

Makes approximately 2 cups

Fresh Pea Hummus

One Easter, I served this fresh pea hummus with a vegetable platter and some crackers. I love this dip, but I stuck it in the den, where during holiday get-togethers, no one goes unless a game is on. The exciting hors d'oeuvres are front and center in the kitchen where people always congregate. At one point, I couldn't find my dad and father-in-law. I looked everywhere, then I found them in the den huddled over the hummus, deep in conversation. I thought they were having a serious business talk and I hesitated to disturb them. Then they saw me, and my dad said, "We're really enjoying this dip. What is it?" I couldn't believe it. They weren't solving the worlds' problems, they found the dip. I now make it for them all the time.

2 cups shelled fresh peas (2 lbs in pods)
3/4 t cumin seeds, toasted*
1/2 cup (packed) cilantro
1 garlic clove, chopped
1/4 cup tahini (sesame paste)
1/2 T lemon juice

- In a small saucepan over high heat simmer peas in salted water until tender, 5 minutes. Drain, reserving liquid and cool
- Grind cumin seeds in a spice grinder or crush with a mortar and pestle. Place cumin, cilantro and garlic in a food processor and pulse to combine. Add peas, tahini and lemon juice and pulse again to combine. Season with salt and pepper to taste. Add 1-2 tablespoons reserved liquid if needed

Makes approximately 2 cups

---

* To toast seeds: place in a skillet over medium heat until fragrant, 5 minutes

Baba Ghanouj

When I was a junior in college, I spent a semester in London. Studying abroad is a rite of passage for many college students, myself included. Sure, the education was important, but to me, it was the first time I felt like an adult on my own in an exciting foreign city. I took on London like a pet project. I had to see, do, and taste it all. I lived in the Kensington area, which was rich in Middle Eastern culture. I loved going into the tiny restaurants, which were everywhere, and sampling whatever caught my eye. It was all so exotic and different from anything I had ever eaten. The Baba Ghanouj was one of my favorites, but I never thought I could make it at home. When I learned the ingredients, I realized it wasn't so hard.

2 lbs eggplant, halved lengthwise
1/4 cup olive oil
1/4 cup tahini (sesame paste)
3 T fresh lemon juice (1-2 lemons)
1 garlic clove, chopped

- Preheat oven to 375°
- Place eggplant cut side down on a rimmed baking sheet lined with non-stick aluminum foil. Roast 45 minutes until eggplants are soft. Cool slightly. Scoop out pulp and place in a strainer over a bowl. Let rest for 30 minutes to drain all liquid
- Place drained eggplant in a food processor. Add oil, tahini, lemon juice and garlic. Process until almost smooth. Season with salt and pepper to taste
- Cover and chill 1 hour

Makes approximately 2 cups

Black Olive Tapenade

Jim and I recently took our first vacation away from the kids, ever! We didn't just go around the corner. We went to Provence in the south of France. Leaving was a little traumatic, but once we got there, we had a very special vacation. We ate, drank, relaxed, and shopped. Shopping in Provence means going to outdoor village markets. Most sell local wares like clothing, pottery, and flowers. But it's the food that left us drooling and the aroma was intoxicating. We'd buy a little of everything, olive tapenade, cheese, baguette and, sausages. Then we'd get a bottle of wine and have a picnic overlooking the Luberon Valley. Here is my American version of black olive tapenade.

1 cup kalamata olives, pitted and halved
1/4 cup (packed) basil
6 anchovy fillets
2 T capers
1 T fresh lemon juice
1/2 garlic clove, minced
1/4 cup olive oil

- In a food processor, pulse olives, basil, anchovies, capers, lemon juice and garlic until coarsely chopped.
- With motor running, slowly add oil until mixture forms a smooth puree
- Cover and chill 1 hour

Makes approximately1 cup

Green Olive Tapenade

Several months ago, Jim and I were at a popular restaurant in New York City having dinner. Along with the bread came a small plate slathered with black olive tapenade on one side and green olive tapenade on the other. We were starving and dug in. Both were amazing. I had never tasted the green version before and I couldn't figure out which one I liked best. When we finished it after contemplating licking the plate, I realized there's a reason why they're served together, they are a perfect match. So, to go with my black olive tapenade, I created a green version and I love to serve them side by side just like the restaurant.

1 cup green olives, pitted and halved
3 anchovy fillets
1 T capers
1/2 garlic clove, minced
1 oz soft goat cheese
2 T olive oil

- In a food processor, pulse olives, anchovies, capers, garlic and cheese until coarsely chopped
- Slowly add olive oil until mixture forms a smooth puree
- Cover and chill 1 hour

Makes approximately 1 cup

43

Chutney Cheddar Spread

I love how everything slows down in the summer. The kids run around the neighborhood playing capture the flag and have lemonade stands. All the windows in the house are open and the house fills with the smell of summer. I practically stop cooking and catch up on all the books I want to read. I do like to be prepared if company stops by and to me, chutney cheese spread screams summer. It requires no cooking and will keep in the refrigerator for several weeks. That way you don't have to turn on the oven or rush to the store. How convenient.

8 oz package of cream cheese
1/2 cup (2 oz) sharp Cheddar cheese, grated
1/4 cup mango chutney
1/2 cup unsalted macadamia nuts

- In a food processor, pulse cheeses, chutney and nuts until blended. Season with salt and pepper to taste
- Cover and chill 1 hour

Makes approximately 2 cups

Stilton Spread

One day I was getting the kids ready to go over to my friend Christina's house for our Friday play group and I was running a little late. When I called to tell her she said, "you better hurry because I made a new hors d'oeuvre and Becky and I are about to finish it." I threw the kids in the car and rushed over. The Stilton spread was delicious and guess who finished it?

8 oz package of cream cheese
1 cup (4 oz) Stilton cheese, crumbled
2 t sherry
dash garlic powder
1/2 cup chopped walnuts, toasted

- In a food processor, pulse cheeses, sherry and garlic powder until blended
- Place in a bowl and fold in walnuts. Cover and chill 1 hour

Makes approximately 1 1/2 cups

Gorgonzola, Scallion & Fresh Mint Spread

As much as I like to cook in the kitchen, I do not like spending time in the garden. I complain about gardening and my brown thumb to anyone who will listen. So when our friends Lorraine and Paul offered to give me some of their mint to plant in our yard, I said thanks but no thanks. I don't need another dead plant on my hands. Paul argued that mint is really a weed and the only nuisance would be containing the growing mint to one spot. So I planted my mint. I was really excited because I love fresh mint and for a while everything I made included my lovely "weed". I created this spread one day after rummaging through my refrigerator. I didn't know if the Gorgonzola would go with the mint, but it turned out to be very tasty and a wonderful summer spread. Oh and by the way, the mint is still thriving in our back yard.

8 oz package of cream cheese, softened
1 cup (4 oz) Gorgonzola cheese, crumbled
4 scallions, trimmed and chopped
2 T fresh mint, chopped

- In a food processor, pulse cream cheeses, scallions and mint until blended
- Cover and chill 1 hour

Makes approximately 1 1/2 cups

<u>Sleigh Ball</u>

If I'm lucky at Christmastime, my friend Tracy will give me one of her famous cheese balls. She always has perfect timing. It's a few days before Christmas and we're all in the holiday spirit. A cheese ball delivered to your doorstep is a reason to drop everything, have a cocktail and enjoy the holidays. This got me thinking about making my own. Not to interfere with Tracy's, I wanted to make one as an hors d'oeuvre on Christmas day. So, I invented the sleigh ball. The inside has a beautiful rosy color thanks to the dried cranberries and the outside is rolled in a mixture of nuts and parsley. When you cut into it, you get the classic Christmas experience. It's a real show stopper and just perfect for the occasion. Thanks for the inspiration, Tracy!

4 oz cream cheese, softened
1/2 cup (2 oz) blue cheese, crumbled
1 t hot sauce
1/2 garlic clove, minced
2 cups (8 oz) sharp Cheddar cheese, grated
1/3 cup dried cranberries
1/4 cup chopped pecans, toasted
1/2 cup flat leaf parsley, chopped

- In a food processor, pulse cream cheese, blue cheese, hot sauce, garlic and Cheddar until combined. Add cranberries and pulse until cranberries are coarsely chopped. Shape mixture into a ball and wrap in plastic wrap
- Chill 2 hours until firm
- In a medium bowl, combine pecans and parsley. Roll cheese ball in mixture to completely cover
- Wrap in plastic and chill until ready to serve

Makes 1 Sleigh Ball

Cold Salmon Mousse with Cucumber Sauce

A long, long time ago, I was at a holiday party at my boss's apartment in New York City. It was a Sunday afternoon and I didn't want to go. My entry-level advertising job was keeping me at the office upwards of 14 hours a day. The last thing I wanted to do was mingle with my co-workers on Sunday. I sat on the couch staring at my watch, waiting to leave at a reasonable hour. On the coffee table staring at me was a cold salmon mousse. It had cucumbers for gills and olives for eyes. It looked as sad as I felt and not a soul had touched it. To look busy, I helped myself. It was delicious. I had some more and it actually lifted my spirits a bit and got me through the party. Many years later, Jim's mom gave me her old recipe for the same thing. I was so excited to make it, except I omitted the decoration and put my cucumbers to better use in the sauce.

Mousse
2 lbs poached salmon (page 150)
or 4 cups canned (4, 7.5 oz cans)
4 T lemon juice (2-3 lemons)
1/3 cup mayonnaise
1 t salt
1/4 t cayenne pepper
1 envelope unflavored gelatin

1 cup heavy cream, whipped
canola oil to grease mold
Cucumber Sauce
8 oz container sour cream
1/2 cup cucumber, peeled,
seeded, and chopped
2 t fresh chives, chopped
1 t fresh dill, chopped

- Mousse: In a food processor, pulse salmon, lemon juice, mayonnaise, salt and cayenne. Dissolve gelatin in 1 cup hot water and combine with salmon mixture. Fold in whipped cream
- Pour into an oiled 1 qt. mold (preferably shaped like a fish). Chill 2 hours until firm
- To serve, place mousse in a hot water bath for approximately 30 seconds. Then, invert onto a serving platter
- Sauce: In a small bowl, combine sour cream, cucumber, chives and dill. Season with salt and pepper to taste. Cover and chill 1 hour
- Serve mousse with sauce on crackers or cocktail pumpernickel bread

Serves 15-20

<u>Soup and Salad</u>

Vegetable Cheddar Soup

When I think about my old life as a working mom versus my life now as a stay-at-home mom, I can honestly say I am far busier now. It's a 24 hour job that never slows down. Many times I can't even have a civilized phone conversation without being interrupted by a needy child. That's why my friend Christina and I have resorted to our 7:00 am phone calls before our kids wake up. One Monday morning she called all excited to tell me about the most amazing soup she had made the night before. It had all kinds of vegetables and four different cheeses. It sounded so good, I made it that Monday night. It was delicious, but what I loved about it was the vegetable combination. I made it the next week with only Cheddar cheese, and I still thought it tasted delicious (and without the expense of buying four different cheeses and only using a little of each).

2 T olive oil
1 medium onion, chopped
1 garlic clove, chopped
1 medium potato, peeled and chopped
1 carrot, peeled and chopped
1 celery stalk, chopped
1 medium zucchini, chopped
48 oz can (6 cups) chicken broth
2 cups (8 oz) Cheddar cheese, grated
1 head of broccoli trimmed and chopped

- In a large stockpot over medium heat sauté onion, garlic, potato, carrot, celery and zucchini in oil until soft, 10 minutes. Add chicken broth and bring to a boil. Reduce heat, cover and simmer, 10 minutes. Add broccoli and simmer until soft, 10 more minutes
- With an immersion blender or in a food processor blend soup until chunky
- Add cheese and stir until melted

Serves 6-8

Broccoli Soup

This soup is from my mother-in-Law, Dottie's repertory. Everyone loves it, so if it's cold outside and we're having dinner at her house, I know she'll make it. The original recipe called for heavy cream, which made it too heavy, so over the years, Dottie experimented. One year she made it with milk, another with yogurt. She finally settled on half and half which Makesit taste just right.

4 T (1/2 stick) unsalted butter
1 leek, trimmed and chopped
1 carrot, peeled and chopped
2 garlic cloves, chopped
32 oz can (4 cups) chicken broth
1 head broccoli, trimmed and chopped
1/2 cup half and half
pinch cayenne pepper
1 t celery seed

- In a medium stockpot over medium heat, sauté leek, carrot and garlic in butter until soft, 5 minutes. Add chicken broth and bring to a boil. Add broccoli, reduce heat and simmer 10 minutes
- Remove from heat and puree with an immersion blender or in a food processor
- Stir in half and half, cayenne, celery seed and salt and pepper to taste

Serves 4-6

Fresh Pea Soup

I first experienced fresh pea soup with my sister-in-law-Christy. We used to sneak away from our advertising jobs in New York City and have lunch in the restaurant of one of the chic department stores in Midtown. We were supposed to be entertaining clients at lunch, so in a sense we were hiding out and catching up. We always ordered the same thing, fresh pea soup and deviled eggs. I couldn't get over how different fresh pea soup tasted from split pea soup. I mean it's all the same vegetable, right? My favorite part of making this soup is getting the kids involved. I plop the bowl of peas in front of them, and they go to work shelling (caution: this can take a long time!). They really enjoy it and are proud to be a part of the cooking process.

1 T olive oil
1 T unsalted butter
1 small onion, chopped
1 celery stalk, chopped
32 oz can (4 cups) chicken broth
(4 cups) shelled fresh peas
(from about 4 lbs unshelled peas)
1/2 cup half and half

- In a medium stockpot, over medium heat, sauté onion and celery in oil and butter until soft, 5 minutes. Add chicken broth and bring to a boil. Add peas, reduce heat and simmer 10 more minutes. Remove from heat
- Puree with an immersion blender or in a food processor, leaving a few peas whole
- Stir in half and half and season with salt and pepper to taste

Serves 4-6

Corn Chowder

My twins used to love corn on the cob until the summer when they lost their two front teeth. So, I cut the corn off the cob, but it just didn't seem the same. They said the corn lost its fun. Then I got creative. I made all kinds of recipes with corn. The one that the children loved the most was corn chowder. It could be 100 degrees outside and they would ask for it. Now, whenever I come across freshly picked corn, I buy it and make corn chowder.

3 1/2 cups (5-6 ears) fresh corn kernels, cobs reserved
4 slices bacon, chopped
2 leeks, trimmed and chopped
3 medium red potatoes, diced
2 cups whole milk
dash hot sauce
2 T flat leaf parsley, chopped
1/4 cup half and half

- In a large stockpot, immerse corncobs in water, bring to a boil, then reduce heat and simmer 20 minutes. Discard corn cobs reserving 4 cups of corn broth
- In same stockpot, cook bacon over medium heat until fat is rendered, 3 minutes. Add leeks and cook until soft, 5 minutes. Add corn broth, milk, potatoes. Cook 15 minutes until potatoes are tender. Add corn and cook 10 more minutes
- Puree half the soup with an immersion blender or in a food processor
- Stir in hot sauce, parsley and half and half. Season with salt and pepper to taste

Serves 6-8

Butternut Squash Soup

When I first started giving dinner parties, I always had the same menu, which helped build my confidence as a cook and hostess. I wasn't inviting the same people to every party, so I always made butternut squash soup followed by beef burgundy. It's a sure thing. The soup actually tastes better if it's made a day ahead, so you have lots of time to do other things the day of the party.

2 medium onions, chopped
3 T unsalted butter
3 cups diced butternut squash
1 granny smith apple, peeled, cored and chopped
3 T flour
1 t curry powder
pinch of nutmeg
3 cups (24oz) chicken broth
1 1/2 cups whole milk

- In large stockpot over medium heat, sauté onions in butter until soft, 5 minutes. Add squash and apple. Sauté until butter is absorbed, 3 minutes, stirring constantly. Add flour, curry powder and nutmeg and cook for 2 more minutes. Add chicken broth and milk. Bring to a boil, and then reduce to a simmer
- Simmer uncovered 15-20 minutes
- Puree soup with an immersion blender or in a food processor. Season with salt and pepper to taste

Serves 4-6

Cucumber-Yogurt Soup

What could be better on a summer day than ice cold soup? I like to make a batch of this delicious soup and keep in the refrigerator to have all week long (lunch, snack, dinner, whatever). It's healthy and filling when you don't feel like having a big hot meal.

3 cups plain low fat yogurt
1 cup (8 oz) chicken broth
1 large cucumber, peeled, seeded and chopped
2 scallions, trimmed and chopped
1 T fresh mint, chopped
1 T fresh cilantro, chopped
1/2 - 1 jalapeno, seeded and chopped
1/2 t salt

- In a food processor, combine all ingredients until almost smooth with a few chunks
- Cover and chill 2 hours

Serves 4-6

Potato Leek Soup

If you ask my daughter, Catie what her favorite food is, she'll tell you potato leek soup. For a long time, she didn't know what a leek was. She thought it was a leak as in faucet. She figured out the double meaning of leeks when she studied homophones in school and was thrilled and relieved. Can you imagine having a favorite food but, for the life of you cannot figure out the meaning of the name? I am so glad that's cleared up for you, Catie!

2 T unsalted butter
4 leeks, trimmed and chopped
1 small onion, chopped
2 medium potatoes, peeled and diced
32 oz can (4 cups) chicken broth
1/4 cup heavy cream
chopped chives and watercress for garnish

- In a medium stockpot over medium heat, sauté leeks and onion in butter, 5 minutes until soft. Add potatoes and cook another 8 minutes. Add broth, and bring to a boil, then reduce to a simmer
- Cover and simmer 20 minutes until potatoes are tender
- Puree soup with an immersion blender or in a food processor
- Stir in cream. Season with salt and pepper to taste
- Garnish with chives and watercress

Serves 4- 6

Stracciatelle with Lemon

When I was working in New York City selling advertising for a national magazine, I was to take clients to lunch. The morning of the lunch date the drill was to call your client to ask their restaurant preference. I did this for a long time, then I got smart. I began deciding on the restaurant based on my careful culinary research and the talk of the town. Nobody seemed to mind. One of my favorites was a little Italian spot on Carmine Street. I looked forward to the stracciatelle soup every time. Here's my version.

48 oz can (6 cups) chicken broth
4 large eggs, lightly beaten
2 T flat leaf parsley, chopped
1/4 cup(1oz) Parmesan cheese, freshly grated
juice and zest of 1 lemon

- In a medium stockpot, bring chicken broth to a boil. Reduce heat to low and keep broth at a gentle simmer
- Slowly drizzle in egg, which will cook as it goes into the simmering broth. Stir soup as the egg is drizzled in
- When all of the egg has been added, stir in lemon juice and zest, cheese and parsley. Season with salt and pepper to taste

Serves 6-8

Spicy Black Bean Soup

Sunday is my favorite day of the week because I cook all day. Jim entertains the kids and I go to it, uninterrupted in the kitchen. I first started doing this when I was working. I'd make all of my weekday meals on Sunday afternoon. Now that I'm home, I have more time to cook during the week, but I still love the focus and the solitude of those quiet afternoons. Nothing is better than a big pot of soup even if we don't eat it that night. Certain soups, like black bean, freeze well. They also tastes better after a few days in the refrigerator. This gives all the flavors a chance to get to know each other.

1 lb (16 oz) dried black beans
2 T olive oil
1 large red onion, chopped
4 oz can diced, green chilies
2 garlic cloves, chopped
1 jalapeno, seeded and chopped
1 T ground cumin
48 oz can (6 cups) chicken broth
1/2 cup (packed) cilantro, chopped
sour cream for garnish

- Place black beans in a pot, cover with water and soak overnight
- Drain in a colander
- In a large stockpot, over medium heat sauté onion, chilies, garlic, jalapeno and cumin until soft, 5 minutes. Add broth and beans and bring to a boil, then cover and reduce to a simmer 1 - 1 1/2 hours, until beans are tender. Season with salt and pepper to taste
- Puree half of the soup with an immersion blender or in a food processor. Stir in cilantro
- Serve with sour cream

Serves 6-8

White Bean Soup with Parmesan

There aren't a lot of things that I come across in a supermarket that completely stump me, but one is Parmesan cheese rinds. I've eaten plenty of Parmesan cheese in my day, but the rind? I came across this recipe and the light bulb went off in my head. Cheese rinds are to be used to flavor a dish, not to actually eat. I've always loved white bean soup and the addition of the rind gives it a greater depth of flavor. I recommend using dried beans, not canned. It's a little more work re-hydrating them, but the superior texture and flavor is worth it.

1 lb (16 oz.) dried great northern beans
3 T olive oil
1 large onion, chopped
1 large carrot, chopped
1 large celery stalk, chopped
48 oz can (6 cups) chicken broth
2 t fresh sage, chopped
2 Parmesan cheese rinds
4 oz (1/4 lb) prosciutto, chopped

- Place beans in a pot, cover and soak overnight
- Drain in a colander
- In a large stockpot over medium heat, sauté onion, carrot and celery in oil until soft, 5 minutes. Add beans, broth, sage, Parmesan rinds and prosciutto. Bring to a boil, then cover and reduce to a simmer. Cook until beans are soft, 1 1/2-2 hours. Add more broth if soup gets too thick
- Remove cheese rinds. Puree half of the soup with an immersion blender or in a food processor. Season with salt and pepper to taste
- Serve with additional freshly grated Parmesan

Serves 6-8

Crab and Avocado Soup

Sometimes a soup can be straightforward and no nonsense like chicken noodle, and sometimes it can be mysterious like crab and avocado. It's the mysterious soup that keeps one interested. You think you know what's in it, but then again, you're not really sure. If you're a cook, it can drive you crazy. Sure, it has crab and avocado but what else? Your guests will be impressed with its complexity and je ne sais quoi? Only you have to know.

2 T unsalted butter
1 small onion, chopped
3 T flour
2, 14 oz cans chicken broth
1/2 cup half and half
2 avocados, peeled, pitted and diced
4 T cilantro, chopped
1 jalapeno, seeded and minced
juice of 1 lime
6 oz fresh crabmeat

- In a medium stockpot over medium heat, sauté onion in butter until soft, 5 minutes. Add flour and stir until absorbed,1 minute. Stir in chicken broth and half and half. Bring soup to a boil, whisking constantly. Reduce to a simmer and cook 5 more minutes
- Add avocado, cilantro, jalapeno and lime juice and puree with an immersion blender or in a food processor
- Add crabmeat and bring to a simmer until crabmeat is heated through. Season to taste with salt and pepper

Serves 4-6

Dad's New England Clam Chowder

The second semester of my freshman year in college, I got dismal grades. I have never to this day heard my father yell at me the way he did then. Luckily, I was spending the summer in Martha's Vineyard and all that yelling was through the pay phone on that lovely island. I rationalized that by the time I got home in August, he would be over it, as he'd have a couple months to remember that his oldest daughter was basically a good kid. That summer on the Vineyard was really fun. One of my discoveries was clam chowder, which is an island specialty. I made it my mission to try it everywhere I went, and I asked for the recipes where I could get them. Here is my version of that delicious summer. I dedicate it to my Dad.

8 oz (1/2 lb) bacon, chopped
2 large leeks, trimmed and chopped
2 garlic cloves, minced
1 T fresh thyme, chopped
2 ears fresh corn kernels
2 medium potatoes, peeled and diced
3, 8 oz bottles clam juice
1 cup heavy cream
1 lb shelled fresh clams

- In a large stockpot over medium/high heat cook bacon until crisp and brown, 8 minutes. Using a slotted spoon, transfer bacon to paper towels to drain. Pour all but 2 tablespoons of the drippings from the pot
- Add leeks, garlic and thyme to pot and sauté until soft, 3 minutes. Add corn and sauté 2 more minutes
- Add potatoes, clam juice and cream. Bring to a boil, reduce heat and simmer and cook 10 minutes. Add clams and bacon and simmer 5 more minutes
- Season with salt and pepper to taste

Serves 4-6

Oyster Stew with Spinach and Sausage

When I was about eight, I loved Saturday lunch at my grandmom & granddads. It would begin with a glass of milk. Grandmom would put exactly two drops of her coffee in it, so we could have coffee together and my milk really did taste like coffee. This cocktail was followed by lunch of oyster stew made by granddad. He made it fresh right before my eyes. I don't remember much more than cream and oysters, and it was delicious. Dessert was my favorite. Ice cream sodas made the old fashioned way with milk, club soda, syrup, ice cream and ice cubes. It was a pretty sophisticated meal for an eight year old. I still love oyster stew. Granddad was a purist, but he was also open to new things. I think he would like this recipe.

1 T canola oil
1 small onion, chopped
1/2 lb chorizo sausage, casing removed
2 cups whole milk
1 1/2 cups half and half
10 oz package baby spinach
1 pint fresh oysters, with their liquor
dash Worcestershire sauce

- In a medium stockpot over medium heat sauté onion in oil until soft, 5 minutes. Add sausage and cook until brown, 10 minutes. Remove sausage/onion mixture and drain on paper towels. Wipe out pot and return sausage/onion mixture
- Add milk and half and half. Continue to cook over medium heat until simmering
- Add spinach and continue simmering, 2 minutes. Add oysters and their liquor and simmer 2 more minutes
- Season with Worcestershire, salt and pepper to taste

Serves 4-6

Roasted Beet and Goat Cheese and Arugula Salad

There's no middle ground when you ask someone if they like beets. They either love them or hate them. I actually never liked beets, until I gave them a chance. I didn't know how easy they were to roast in the oven, or how flavorful they are totally plain. Put them together with goat cheese and arugula and it's a perfect marriage!

2 large beets, trimmed
1/2 shallot, minced
1/2 T white wine vinegar
juice of 1/2 lemon
2 T olive oil
2 oz (1/2 cup) goat cheese, crumbled
2 bunches arugula, washed and chopped

- Preheat oven to 400°
- Wrap beets individually in aluminum foil. Bake until tender, 1 hour. Cool, then peel, slice and set aside
- In a small bowl, whisk together vinegar, mustard and shallot. Slowly add olive oil, whisking to emulsify. Season with salt and pepper to taste
- Toss with arugula, beets and cheese

Serves 4-6

Baby Greens with Warm Goat Cheese

When Jim and I were dating, we were invited to a dinner party given by my friend, Alex. She lived in a typical New York City, closet-size apartment that could fit about one guest. So, she borrowed a friend's very cool loft in Soho for the party. Alex was organized with her meal and everything was carefully prepared before hand. Then, just before we sat down, she pulled out a big log of goat cheese, sliced it with dental floss, which is a trick to slicing goat cheese in perfect discs, and she fried it, just like that. I thought she was so courageous to cook while her guests were waiting for dinner. But, it was fun watching her and the finished salad was amazing.

2 large egg whites
12 oz log goat cheese, chilled and sliced into discs with dental floss
3/4 cup bread crumbs (panko*)
2 T apple cider vinegar
2 T Dijon mustard
pinch sugar
1/4 olive oil + 2 T
10 oz package mesculin greens

- In a small bowl, whisk together egg whites and 2 teaspoons of water. Dip cheese rounds in egg then dredge in bread crumbs, pressing lightly to adhere. Place on a baking sheet and chill 15 minutes
- Dressing: In a small bowl, whisk vinegar, mustard, sugar. Add 1/4 cup olive oil in a slow stream whisking until emulsified. Season with salt and pepper to taste. Set aside
- Heat remaining 2 tablespoons oil in a large skillet over medium high heat. Sauté cheese 30 seconds per side
- Toss greens with dressing and top with goat cheese

Serves 4-6

---

* Japanese breadcrumbs

Hearts of Lettuce with Gorgonzola Vinaigrette

Every summer as a child, the night before I left for overnight camp, my parents would take us to the best restaurant on the Jersey shore for one last "real meal". It was always a magical night. My brothers and I were so excited to go back to camp to see our friends. My parents knew the owner of the restaurant and we were treated like royalty. I always got the same meal starting with this salad. It was my first salad beyond iceberg lettuce. This is my version.

2 T white wine vinegar
1 t Dijon mustard
1 shallot, chopped
1 t coarse salt
1/4 t freshly ground pepper
6 T olive oil
1/3 cup (2 1/2 oz) crumbled Gorgonzola cheese
2 heads of Boston lettuce

- In a small bowl, whisk vinegar, mustard, shallot, salt and pepper. Add olive oil in a slow stream whisking until emulsified. Fold in Gorgonzola
- Tear lettuce into bite size pieces and pour dressing on top

Serves 4-6

Buttermilk Blue Cheese Dressing
over Iceberg Wedges

My friends and I loved the night life when we were single living in New York City. There was a restaurant near my apartment on the Upper East Side that was open all hours. After many a late night, my friends Carol, Abby and I would stumble into the place. It was always packed at 2 am and the service was slow. Luckily, sitting on every table was a big bowl of iceberg lettuce wedges accompanied by four different creamy salad dressings. I always had the blue cheese, which at 2 am was delicious. I never forgot that salad. Here's my version.

1/2 cup mayonnaise
1/3 cup (1 1/2 oz) blue cheese, crumbled
1/4 cup plain nonfat yogurt
3 T buttermilk
2 T white wine vinegar
2 scallions trimmed and chopped
1 head of iceberg lettuce

- Dressing: whisk mayonnaise, blue cheese, yogurt, buttermilk and vinegar in a small bowl until smooth. Fold in scallions. Season with salt and pepper to taste
- Cut lettuce in 4-6 wedges
- Pour dressing evenly over lettuce

Serves 4-6

Cobb Salad

The first time I ever had a Cobb salad, I couldn't believe how good it was. All of my favorite things on top of lettuce. This is what I call a meal salad as opposed to an accompaniment to a meal. If your organized with your ingredients, it's easy to put together.

1 lb skinless, boneless chicken breast
2, 14 oz cans chicken broth
2 large eggs
1 head romaine lettuce cut into 1" pieces
1 bunch watercress, chopped
6 slices bacon, cooked, drained and crumbled
1 avocado, pitted, peeled and diced
1/2 cup (2 oz) blue cheese, crumbled
2 tomatoes, seeded and chopped
3 T red wine vinegar
1 t Dijon mustard
1 T olive oil

- In a medium saucepan over medium/high heat, poach chicken in broth, 15 minutes. Discard broth, cool chicken and cube. Set aside
- Place eggs in a small saucepan, cover with water by 1". Bring to a boil. Turn off heat, cover and let stand 15 minutes. Cool, peel, chop and set aside
- Place lettuces in a big bowl
- Arrange chicken, eggs, bacon, avocado, cheese and tomatoes like pie slices
- Dressing: In a small bowl whisk vinegar, mustard and oil. Season with salt and pepper to taste and drizzle over salad

Serves 4-6

Caesar Salad

Every family has a few culinary traditions, whether it's a holiday meal together, summer cookout, or birthday dinner. In our family, the birthday dinner is king. You can have whatever you want on your special day. Jim always requests a homemade Caesar salad right down to the croutons. It's a little labor intensive, but I don't mind because I get to eat it too.

2 garlic cloves
1/8 t coarse salt
4 T olive oil
half a loaf French baguette (about 1/4 lb), cut into 1" cubes
2 anchovies
juice of 1/2 lemon
1 t Worcestershire sauce
1/2 t Dijon mustard
1/4 t freshly ground pepper
2 heads romaine lettuce, cut into 1" pieces
3/4 cup (3 oz) Parmesan cheese, freshly grated

- Preheat oven to 350°
- In a medium bowl, mash 1 garlic clove with the salt to form a smooth paste. Whisk in 1 tablespoon of olive oil. Add bread and toss to combine. Spread in a single layer on a rimmed baking sheet. Bake 20 minutes until golden brown, turning once. Set aside
- Dressing: in a small bowl mash 1 garlic clove with the anchovies to form a smooth paste. Whisk in lemon juice, Worcestershire, mustard and pepper. Slowly whisk in remaining oil until emulsified.
- In a large serving bowl toss lettuce, dressing and croutons. Sprinkle half of Parmesan cheese and toss again.
- Sprinkle remaining Parmesan cheese on top and serve

Serves 4-6

Panzanella

When my sister-in-law was working at a trendy magazine in New York City, her editor in chief once used her pull to get us a dinner reservation at the new Italian restaurant in town. There were eight of us, Christy, Jim's parents, brother Peter and us spouses all crammed around a rustic farm table ordering salad and pasta priced out of the stratosphere. I ordered the panzanella salad to start and asked for some shavings of Parmesan cheese on top. The waiter looked at me in disgust and walked away. Seconds later, the owner appeared who, in no uncertain terms, informed me that one never puts cheese on a panzanella salad. My table stared at me in horror. Did I just embarrass the entire Currie family? Or was this chef/owner a little nutty? Luckily, when he walked away, our table started quietly giggling, then outright laughing. No, I would not be ex-communicated from the family that night but, they do love to tease me about my "faux pas" when we go out to dinner.

8 thick cut slices Italian bread, cubed
2 tomatoes, seeded and chopped
1 small cucumber, peeled,
seeded and chopped
1 small red onion, chopped
1 cup (packed) basil, chopped

1/2 cup olive oil + 1 T
3 T balsamic vinegar
fresh Parmesan
shavings for garnish

- Preheat oven to 350°
- Place bread cubes on a baking sheet and toss with 1 tablespoon olive oil. Bake until toasted, 10 minutes. Set aside
- In a medium bowl combine tomato, cucumber, onion and basil. Drizzle with oil and vinegar and season with salt and pepper to taste. Toss well
- Place half the bread in a serving bowl, spoon half the vegetable mixture over it. Repeat with remaining ingredients. Cover and chill 1 hour
- Toss salad and top with Parmesan shavings and serve

Serves 4-6

Tex Mex Chopped Salad

Every summer our neighborhood has a block party. We close off the street with barricades, bring out tables, chairs, and grills and catch up with our neighbors. All 40 neighborhood kids get to ride their bikes in the street without looking both ways. It's simple fare, hamburgers and hot dogs for the most part, although at least one family usually pulls out steaks. Even number houses bring salad to share and odd number houses bring dessert to share. One year I forgot to prepare my salad until hours before the party started. We were leaving for vacation and I had nothing in the house. I rummaged through the refrigerator and put everything I could find in my big plastic bowl and voila! Tex mex salad was born.

15 oz can black beans, drained
2 cups fresh corn kernels, cooked (4 ears)
1 head iceberg lettuce, chopped
2 tomatoes, seeded and chopped
2 cups (8 oz) Monterey Jack cheese, grated
juice of 2 limes
1/4 cup extra virgin olive oil

- In a large serving bowl combine beans, corn, lettuce, tomato and cheese. Toss well to combine
- Add lime juice and oil. Season with salt and pepper to taste
- Toss again to combine

Serves 8-10

Avocado, Tomato, and Cucumber Salad

I hate wasting food and try not to do it. If I have something in the refrigerator that I know cannot last another day, I'll create a meal around it. That's how I came up with this salad. It was Thursday night and we were going away for the weekend. I knew the avocado, tomato and cucumber on the countertop would not make it until Monday. I chopped it up, threw it in a bowl, whipped up a little dressing and made a salad that Jim declared a "keeper".

1 avocado, pitted and chopped
1 large tomato, seeded and chopped
1 large cucumber, peeled, seeded and chopped

Dressing:
1 shallot, minced
juice of 1 lime
1 T olive oil
1/2 t honey
salt and pepper

- In a medium bowl, combine avocado, tomato and cucumber
- In a small bowl, whisk all dressing ingredients
- Toss with vegetables
- Season with salt and pepper to taste

Serves 4

Vegetables and Side Dishes

Roasted Sugar Snap Peas

I used to steam my sugar snap peas, which was fine until one day I was broiling chicken and I threw the peas under the broiler because of convenience. They turned out so delicious that now I only broil them. It takes less than five minutes from beginning to end. If I have fresh chives, I like to sprinkle them on top for a subtle extra kick, although you don't have to.

1 1/2 lbs sugar snap peas
1 T olive oil
coarse salt
2 T fresh chives, chopped

- Preheat broiler.
- Toss peas with oil on a foil-lined rimmed baking sheet. Broil 2 minutes until bright green and crisp tender, tossing once with a spatula
- Transfer to a serving bowl and sprinkle with salt and chives

Serves 6-8

Balsamic Roasted Carrots

There is nothing more annoying than planning a meal for a family dinner or dinner party and realizing that every dish looks the same. Sometimes while cooking, you have the most perfect dish that lacks in any distinguishable color. Luckily there are carrots to brighten up any meal. These are basic roasted carrots with a little splash of balsamic vinegar.

2 lbs carrots, peeled and cut into match stick size pieces (caution! this can be time consuming)
2 T olive oil
1/4 t salt
2 T balsamic vinegar

- Preheat oven to 425°
- Toss carrots with oil and salt on a foil-lined rimmed baking sheet. Roast carrots, stirring occasionally until tender, 20-25 minutes
- Remove from oven, drizzle vinegar over carrots and toss. Continue roasting carrots until most of vinegar is evaporated, 2 minutes

Serves 6-8

Sautéed Zucchini with Basil

The combination of zucchini and basil make a perfect pair, especially in the summer, when both are at their freshest. A word of caution: If you overcook zucchini, they turn translucent and soggy.

1/4 cup olive oil
2 1/2 lbs (about 5) zucchini
1/2 cup (packed) basil, chopped

- Cut zucchini into matchstick size pieces (caution! This can be time consuming)
- In large skillet over high sauté zucchini in oil until tender, 5 minutes, stirring constantly
- Transfer to a bowl and toss with basil. Season with salt and pepper to taste

Serves 6-8

Broccoli Puree

Getting kids to eat vegetables can be, well, challenging to say the least. In our house, our kids have negotiated their veggie allotment to one raw baby carrot per dinner. At least they're eating something. It doesn't always have to be boring, though. My kids love broccoli soup, so I created a broccoli puree with similar ingredients. The kids love it and I do too.

1 1/2 t olive oil
1 medium onion, chopped
1 garlic clove, chopped
1/2 cup heavy cream
2 lbs broccoli, trimmed and chopped
1/2 t celery seed
dash cayenne pepper

- In a medium saucepan over medium heat sauté onion and garlic in oil until soft, 5 minutes. Add cream and bring to a boil stirring constantly until slightly thickened. Turn off heat and set aside
- In a medium stockpot, boil broccoli in salted water until very tender, 8-10 minutes. Drain in a colander
- Place cream mixture and broccoli in a food processor. Add celery seed and cayenne pepper. Puree until smooth. Season with salt and pepper to taste

Serves 4-6

Marinated, Grilled Asparagus

As much as I love to cook, I don't like to grill. The heat is hard to gauge and I can never tell if anything is done. Luckily, my husband Jim has a sixth sense with the grill. He rarely over or undercooks anything. I'm still trying to figure out how he does it. He's an expert with grilled asparagus, which is not easy. For one thing, they can burn while you're flipping a steak right before your eyes. Thanks to Jim, I know that will never happen in our house.

3 T balsamic vinegar
2 T fresh lemon juice
1 T olive oil
1 T soy sauce
1 1/2 lb asparagus, trimmed

- Pre-heat grill to medium heat
- Combine vinegar, lemon juice, olive oil and soy sauce in a large zip-top bag. Add asparagus and marinate 30 minutes
- Remove asparagus and discard marinade. Place on grill and cook until slightly charred, 5-10 minutes depending on thickness (Can also be broiled in the oven)

Serves 4-6

Spinach Au Gratin

Vegetable dishes have different personalities, and you set your expectations before your first bite. Spinach au gratin is the dish with the big personality. It's rich, indulgent and easy to love. It's perfect for a big family holiday dinner, and will get a lot of attention on the buffet table.

3, 10 oz bags baby spinach
2 T unsalted butter
1 small onion, chopped
2 garlic cloves, minced
1/2 t cayenne pepper
2 cups (8 oz) Cheddar cheese, grated
1 cup bread crumbs (panko*)

- In a large stockpot over medium/high heat, toss spinach until completely wilted, 5 minutes. Wrap in a kitchen towel and twist to drain as much liquid as possible. Set aside
- Preheat oven to 400°
- In a medium pot, over medium heat sauté onion and garlic in butter until soft, 5 minutes. Add spinach and cook 3 minutes. Turn off heat. Add cheese and stir until melted
- Season with cayenne and salt and pepper to taste and spread into a 9" square baking dish
- Sprinkle with bread crumbs pressing in a little and bake 20-25 minutes until lightly brown

Serves 6-8

---

* Japanese breadcrumbs

Chopped Spinach with Toasted Sesame Seeds

In our family, like most, the weekdays are deliriously hectic. The kids are busy with school, homework, sports, and more homework. I never know if Jim will be coming home early or late from work until he walks in the door. In the middle of all the chaos, I take a firm stand in the notion that the day should end with a home cooked meal. We may not all eat together at the end of the day, but it will always be a healthy, well balanced dinner. This spinach side dish is perfect for a busy week night. It's easy, healthy, and most important, tasty.

1/4 cup sesame seeds
2, 10 oz bags baby spinach
4 t sesame oil
2 T seasoned rice vinegar
dash hot sauce

- To toast sesame seeds: Place in skillet over medium heat. Toast until golden, 5 minutes. Set aside
- In a large stockpot, over medium/high heat, toss spinach until wilted, 3 minutes. Wrap in a kitchen towel and twist to drain out as much liquid as possible. Transfer to a work surface and chop coarsely
- Place in a serving bowl, add sesame oil, vinegar and hot sauce (omit hot sauce if serving to children). Season with salt and pepper to taste and sprinkle with sesame seeds

Serves 4-6

Wilted Spinach

If you're having a dinner party and you really want to impress your guests, serve wilted spinach. How boring you say? Not this recipe. I use it as a base (a mattress, if you will) under meat, chicken, pork, or fish. Wilted spinach is a good match with any main dish and it looks great too. Be careful of overcooking. When just wilted, spinach has a beautiful, vibrant green color. If you cook it a minute too long, it turns a nasty shade of olive green.

2 T olive oil
1 garlic clove, minced
2, 10 oz bags baby spinach
1/2 t nutmeg (optional)

- In a large stockpot over low heat, sauté garlic in oil 2-3 minutes (make sure garlic does not burn)
- Add spinach, tossing until just wilted, 3 minutes
- Sprinkle with nutmeg, salt and pepper to taste. Toss again and serve

Serves 4-6

Roasted Vegetables

There is nothing better than a big platter of freshly roasted vegetables. Almost any vegetable will do, and it's a hard dish to ruin. This recipe calls for easy to find vegetables, but you can use whatever you like or any that are in season. Just make sure you have about a total of 4 lbs.

1 lb carrots, 1" cubes
1 lb squash or zucchini, 1"cubes
1 large potato, 1"cube (about 1 lb)
2 medium red onions cut into 8 wedges (about 1 lb)
3 T olive oil
1 1/2 t coarse salt
1/2 t freshly ground pepper
2 T chopped fresh parsley

- Preheat oven to 400°
- Combine carrots, squash or zucchini, potatoes, onions, olive oil, salt and pepper in two foil-lined rimmed baking sheets
- Roast for 30-40 minutes, turning half way through
- Add parsley, and toss to coat

Serves 8-10

Fabulous Potatoes

Many years ago we were at a dinner party at our good friends Amy and
Carmine's house. Amy used to work with my husband, Jim, and the
guests were mostly from their office. I was newly pregnant with
William and feeling horrible. Not a lot of food appealed to me, but
when Amy served the potatoes, they looked and smelled amazing. After
eating them, I felt better than I had in weeks. When I asked her for the
recipe, she laughed and said they're called fabulous potatoes and
hesitated to tell me the calorie-laden recipe. But I persisted because,
hey, I was pregnant and all I know is that they really are fabulous.

1 cup (2 sticks) unsalted butter
1 medium onion, chopped
2 lb bag frozen hash brown potatoes
16 oz container sour cream
10 3/4 oz can cream of chicken soup
2 cups (8 oz) Cheddar cheese, grated
2 cup corn flakes, crushed

- Preheat oven to 350°
- In a large stockpot over medium heat, sauté onion in 1 stick of
  butter until soft, 5 minutes. Add potatoes and stir to combine.
  Turn off heat and add sour cream, soup (undiluted) and cheese.
  Stir to combine
- Pour into a 13x9" baking dish (At this point can be made and
  refrigerated up to one day in advance)
- Melt remaining butter and pour over corn flakes in a bowl.
  Sprinkle mixture over potatoes
- Bake 1 hour, uncovered until brown and bubbly

Serves 8-10

Fabulous Rice

Having a recipe like "Fabulous Potatoes" for a dinner party is, well, fabulous. But I just couldn't keep making the same potato dish for every party. Especially since it wasn't even my recipe. I was explaining this dilemma to my mother -in -law one day, and she told me about a rice dish that she remembered having years ago. After a little digging, she located the recipe. I never got the name, but I call it fabulous rice because it too is fabulous.

1 cup fine egg noodles
1 cup (2 sticks) unsalted butter
2 cups long grain rice
2, 10 1/2 oz cans onion soup
2, 14 oz cans chicken broth
1 T soy sauce
8 oz can sliced water chestnuts, drained

- Preheat oven to 350º
- In a medium saucepan over medium/high heat, sauté uncooked noodles in butter until toasted, 5 minutes. Place noodles in a 13x9" baking dish
- Add rice, both soups (undiluted), soy sauce and water chestnuts to noodles and stir to combine (at this point, can be made and refrigerated up to one day in advance)
- Bake 1 hour, uncovered until brown and bubbly

Serves 8-10

Mini Baked Potatoes with Sea Salt

Most Sundays in the summer, we take family outing to the farmers market in town. Local farmers take over the bank parking lot and sell everything from fresh wild flowers to homemade mozzarella to just picked fruits and vegetables. One of my favorite merchants has perfectly round, smooth, golden potatoes about the size of golf balls. They're too perfect to cut up or mash. So I came up with this mini baked potato recipe that presents them beautifully. Since there are so few ingredients, the key is high quality and freshness. Really good extra virgin olive oil and coarse fleur de sel are the most flavorful to cook with.

2 lbs small creamer potatoes, scrubbed
1/2 cup best quality olive oil
coarse salt

- Preheat oven to 450°
- Pierce potatoes with a fork. Arrange on the oven rack and bake 1-1 1/2 hours until hard and crisp when tapped with a fork
- Using a serrated knife, split the potatoes without cutting them all the way through
- Drizzle with olive oil and sprinkle with salt

Serves 6-8

Kristen's Potatoes

One lazy August Sunday, we were at the swim club enjoying the afternoon. It was quiet and peaceful, as opposed to July when every other kid in town is in the pool creating serious bedlam. My friend Kristen was describing a potato dish she had made up and cooked all the time with no name, no identity. What struck me was how she described the potatoes: Really crispy, cheesy and garlicky. Even Jim put down his newspaper to listen. Intrigued, I went home to re-create the recipe. It was really good and goes with everything. Best of all, Kristen told me, the leftovers taste even better and crispier re-heated the next day.

2 1/2 lbs fingerling potatoes cut in half
4 garlic cloves, minced
1/2 cup olive oil
1/2 cup Parmesan cheese, freshly grated
1 cup bread crumbs (panko*)

- Preheat oven to 400°
- In a large bowl, toss potatoes with oil. Combine garlic, cheese and bread crumbs and toss with potatoes
- Pour in a 13x9" baking dish
- Bake 45 minutes, turning every 15 until crispy and golden brown

Serves 6-8

---

* Japanese breadcrumbs

Oven Baked Fries

One of the great joys of motherhood is watching your children eat. You know you're providing sustenance and nourishment, helping them grow, keeping them healthy. When one of my kids requests a certain dish or meal I am happy to oblige. But, one thing I will never make for them is anything deep fried. Deep frying at home is greasy and smelly, not to mention unhealthy. I have no problem with them ordering French fries, mozzarella sticks, or fried chicken in a restaurant, but it's not happening at home. This doesn't mean they have to be deprived at home, though. These oven baked fries are so good because of the combination of butter and oil. They're cooked at a very high heat keeping the inside light and fluffy and the outside crispy.

2 lbs fingerling potatoes, cut into wedges
1 T vegetable oil
2 T unsalted butter, melted
coarse salt

- Preheat oven to 550°, or highest setting
- In a large bowl, toss potatoes with oil and melted butter. Spread in a single layer on a foil lined rimmed baking sheet. Bake 15- 20 minutes, turning once until golden all over
- Season with salt to taste (For an English version, sprinkle with malt vinegar)

Serves 4-6

Potato and Onion Gratin

I'm always looking for a good potato casserole dish. Striking the right
balance of potato, milk or cream, and seasoning can make a very
satisfying side dish to almost any type of meat, chicken, or fish. This
gratin is delicious because the potatoes and onions are so
complimentary. It's a little on the rich side, but worth every bite.

2 lbs (about 6) Yukon Gold potatoes, thinly sliced
1 T fresh rosemary, chopped
1 T fresh thyme, chopped
1 large onion, thinly sliced
3 T unsalted butter, in small pieces
1 cup heavy cream
1 cup whole milk
salt and pepper

- Preheat oven to 400°
- Layer 1/4 of potatoes in 13x9" baking dish. Season with salt and
  pepper. Sprinkle rosemary and thyme. Layer 1/3 of onions and
  dot with butter. Repeat same combination until everything is
  layered, finishing with a potato layer
- Combine heavy cream and milk and pour over potatoes
- Bake for 1 hour until bubbly and golden
- Let rest for 10 minutes before serving

Serves 6-8

Horseradish Mashed Potatoes

I have to admit, I do not like mashed potatoes. Everyone in my family loves them, so this creates a problem whether it's a weeknight dinner or a family gathering because I tend to not make them. So, for those of you who like mashed potatoes, this is actually a very good and simple recipe. If you want to be totally traditional or if you're serving to children, omit the horseradish. If you're having a dinner party, the horseradish version is very impressive.

2 lbs potatoes, peeled and quartered
1 cup half and half
3 T unsalted butter
2 T drained, bottled horseradish

- In a large pot, cover potatoes with salted, cold water by 1 inch. Bring to boil, then reduce to a simmer and cook uncovered 25 minutes until tender. Drain in a colander
- In a small saucepan, heat half and half and butter to simmering. Turn off heat, cover and set aside
- Meanwhile, place drained potatoes back in the pot and mash with a potato masher. Add hot milk mixture and stir. Add horseradish and stir again.
- Season with salt and pepper to taste

Serves 4-6

Summer Potato Salad

Nothing says summer like traditional potato salad. There are all kinds of versions and everyone has their own special recipe. I love this one because of a little trick that gives them a great depth of flavor. Right after the potatoes are cooked and still warm, add a little vinegar. The potatoes will absorb the liquid and become slightly tangy. I also saw a recipe once, which added the juice from the pickle jar. That sounds intriguing to me, but I'll stick with vinegar.

2 1/2 lbs potatoes, peeled and cubed
3 T apple cider vinegar
5 large hard boiled eggs
1 cup mayonnaise
2 T Dijon mustard
1 small onion, chopped
3 celery stalks, chopped
1/4 cup chopped dill pickle

- In a large stockpot, boil potatoes in salted water, about 20 minutes. Drain in a colander and place in a large bowl and toss with vinegar
- In a small bowl, mash egg yolks (reserving whites) and mix in mayonnaise, mustard and onion
- Chop egg whites and celery and gently toss with pickle, potatoes and mayonnaise mixture in a large serving bowl
- Season with salt and pepper to taste

Serves 8-10

Mediterranean Baked Couscous and Spinach

One of the things that I love about living in the suburbs is the wonderful sense of community. Just having your child in school opens the door to so many opportunities to get involved, whether it's a guest reader in class or lunch with other parents. It was at one of these "potluck" luncheons that I came across this terrific dish. The larger "Israeli" or "Grande" couscous works better with the other ingredients versus of the smaller "Moroccan" style.

1 cup couscous (Israeli version)
14 oz can chicken broth
10 oz package frozen, chopped spinach, thawed and squeezed dry
14 oz can artichoke hearts, drained and quartered
4 oz container (1 cup) crumbled feta cheese*
1/3 cup pine nuts, toasted

- Preheat oven to 350°
- In a medium saucepan, simmer couscous in chicken broth, covered, 10 minutes.
- Combine with spinach, artichokes and feta cheese. Place mixture in a 9" square baking dish. Top with pine nuts
- Bake 20 minutes

Serves 6-8

---

* Gorgonzola cheese can be substituted for feta

Polenta with Gorgonzola and Spinach

Every winter there is usually at least one really bad snow storm where school is closed for several days. The first day is so exciting. The world looks beautiful all dressed in white. The kids play outside until they're numb, and then come in for hot chocolate with giant marshmallows. The second snow day is still magical. By the third day, insanity sets in. The roads are plowed so you cannot for the life of you understand why there is no school. By now I haven't been to the gym in days and my kids sense it, so they cut a wide path around me. Well, its days like this when you need some good old fashioned comfort food. Yes, it's a side dish and I absolutely recommend it for a dinner party. But, nothing Makesme happier when I'm stuck at home on a winter day than a big bowl of polenta with Gorgonzola and spinach. Then I can go out and shovel some more snow.

32 oz can (4 cups) chicken broth
1 garlic clove, minced
2 t fresh rosemary, chopped
1 1/2 cups polenta
5 oz bag baby spinach
1/2 cup heavy cream
4 oz container (1 cup) crumbled Gorgonzola cheese

- In a medium saucepan over medium/high heat, combine chicken broth, garlic, rosemary and polenta and bring to a boil.
- Add spinach and stir until wilted. Add cream and stir until absorbed. Turn off heat, add cheese and stir until melted.
- Season with salt and pepper to taste

Serves 4-6

<u>Vidalia Onion Bread Pudding</u>

Planning a menu for a dinner party can be challenging. It all has to work from hors d'oeuvres to dessert. Sometimes all it takes is one interesting dish to pull an otherwise average meal together. This bread pudding is that dish. Because it's so rich, it works best with simply grilled or roasted meat, or chicken and a sautéed vegetable. Don't be fooled by the onion. Vidalia is very mild and gets sweeter as it cooks. Combined with the cheeses, your guests will be begging for more.

1 T unsalted butter
1 T olive oil
2 Vidalia onions, chopped
3 cups whole milk
1/4 cup white wine
1 T fresh thyme
1 t salt
1/4 t freshly ground black pepper
3 large eggs, lightly beaten

1/2 French baguette cut into
1" cubes
1 1/2 cup (6 oz) Gruyere cheese, freshly grated
3/4 cup (3 oz) Parmesan cheese, freshly grated

- Preheat oven to 400°
- In a large skillet over medium heat, sauté onions in butter and olive oil for 30 minutes until browned, stirring often.
- Meanwhile, place bread cubes in the bottom of a 13x9" baking dish. Sprinkle 1 cup of Gruyere and 1/2 cup Parmesan cheese
- In a medium bowl, whisk milk, eggs, thyme, salt and pepper
- Pour mixture over bread and cheese pushing bread down to absorb liquid.
- When onions are cooked, arrange on top, followed by remaining cheese. (At this point, can be made and refrigerated up to one day in advance).
- Bake 30 minutes until golden and set.

Serves 8-10

<u>Pasta</u>

Oven Baked Rigatoni

Halloween in our neighborhood is celebrated as much if not more than any other holiday. Everyone gets in the spirit and decorates their homes and yards but, one house in particular outdoes itself every year. Mike spends weeks transforming his front yard into an authentic haunted house. Our kids pretend they aren't afraid until Halloween night when they have to walk through the scary haunted scenes to get their treat. Ellen buys about 1,000 full size candy bars to make it worth their while. Jim stands at the curb while they go in and they're relieved to see their dad when they return. I man our front door with my "fun size" candy bars. Yep, I'm cheap, but last Halloween, I counted over 500 visitors. Trick or treating is an all night affair. The kids set out just after dark and are at it until well after 8:00. I make a big dish of rigatoni, so it's ready when they need to come in for refueling. It's become a Halloween tradition that my kids fondly re-named riga-bony.

2 lbs Italian sausage, casings removed
1 T olive oil
1 garlic clove, minced
1 small onion, chopped
6 oz can tomato paste
2, 28 oz cans crushed tomatoes in puree

1 lb rigatoni,
cooked and drained
1 lb mozzarella cheese,
grated
15 oz container ricotta
cheese

- Preheat oven to 350°
- In a medium skillet over medium heat, cook sausage, stirring frequently to break up into small pieces, 10 minutes. Drain on paper towels and set aside
- In a large saucepan over medium heat, sauté garlic and onion in oil until soft, 5 minutes. Add tomato paste and cook 2 more minutes. Add tomatoes and simmer uncovered, 15 minutes. Season with salt and pepper to taste. Set aside
- In a medium bowl combine ricotta and half the mozzarella. Season with salt and pepper to taste
- In a 13x9" baking dish, spread 1/3 of the sauce, then half the rigatoni, half the ricotta mixture, and half the sausage. Repeat with 1/3 sauce, remaining rigatoni, ricotta mixture and sausage. Top with remaining sauce and mozzarella cheese

- Bake 40 minutes until bubbly

Serves 8-10

Lasagna

Getting invited as a family to a party is exciting and quite brave for the hostess, for it can get chaotic (not to mention messy). Let's look at the circumstances: First, most families consist of a couple kids. Invite five families and you could easily have 15 junior guests. Second, kids are tired at dinnertime and you never know when one will blow. It's a potentially embarrassing situation. Third, the parents aren't really paying attention to the kids because we're having our own party, so the house gets trashed. As a guest it's a great night out, but I always leave feeling a little guilty because I know the host and hostess have several hours of clean-up ahead of them. I know this from my own experiences. However, if you are game to host a family party, lasagna is the perfect dish to serve. Parents and kids alike love it. Toss a green salad and add chocolate chip cookies for dessert and you're set.

Sauce:
1/2 lb(8 oz) pancetta, diced
1 medium onion, chopped
4 garlic cloves, minced
1 1/2 cups red wine
2, 28 oz cans plum tomatoes
3 T tomato paste
1 lb Italian sausage, casing removed
Meatballs
1 lb lean ground beef
1/4 cup (1 oz) Parmesan cheese, freshly grated
2 large eggs
1/4 cup flat leaf parsley, chopped
1/2 cup flour
2 T olive oil

Lasagna:
15 oz container ricotta cheese
2 large eggs
2 cups Parmesan cheese freshly grated
1/2 cup flat leaf parsley, chopped
4 cups (1 lb) mozzarella cheese, grated
1 lb oven ready lasagna noodles

- Sauce: In a large stockpot over medium heat, cook pancetta until brown and crispy, 10 minutes. Drain on paper towels and discard all but 1 tablespoon of grease
- In same stockpot, sauté onion and 2 garlic cloves in pancetta drippings until soft, 5 minutes. Add wine and cook until mostly

reduced, 10 minutes. Add tomatoes and crush with a wooden spoon. Then add tomato paste and two cups water. Bring to a boil, then cover, reduce to a simmer and cook for 2 1/2hours

- While the sauce is cooking, brown sausage until crispy and cooked through. Drain on paper towels and add to sauce
- Meatballs: combine beef, cheese, eggs, parsley and 2 garlic cloves. Season with salt and pepper. Shape into meatballs and dust lightly with flour
- Heat 2 tablespoons oil in a skillet and brown meatballs on all sides. (They do not need to be cooked through) Add to sauce
- Lasagna: Combine ricotta, eggs, Parmesan, parsley and all but 1 cup mozzarella. Season with salt and pepper and mix well. Set aside
- Meanwhile, after 2 1/2hours, remove sauce from heat. Pre-heat oven to 350°
- Take out meatballs, slice and set aside. Spoon sauce to cover bottom of a 13x9" baking dish. Add a layer of noodles then cheese then meatballs then sauce. Repeat until everything is used up. Top with remaining 1 cup mozzarella
- Bake 30 minutes until bubbly
- Let rest 10 minutes before serving

Serves 8-10

Penne with Tomato and Basil

The local women's club in town raises money all year long for various community projects. I'm delighted to be a member because of the good work and friendships that I've formed. Every fall, to kick off the season, there's a pot luck supper. Members are given recipes to cook and bring to the event. One year it was an Italian theme and this penne dish is what I brought. It was so delicious, I started making it all the time.

3 T olive oil
1 medium onion, chopped
2 garlic cloves, chopped
1 cup half and half
3/4 cup chicken broth
1 1/2 lbs plum tomatoes, seeded and chopped

1 1/2 cups (packed) basil, chopped
1 lb penne pasta, cooked and drained

- In a large skillet, over medium heat, sauté onion in olive oil until soft, 5 minutes. Add garlic and stir 1 minute. Add half and half and broth. Bring to a boil until thickened, 5 minutes. Add basil and cook 1 minute. Add tomatoes and cook 2 minutes. Season with salt and pepper to taste
- Toss with pasta

Serves 4-6

Winter Tomato Sauce

This is one of those sauces that you can start making Sunday morning and cook it all day. When I make it, we usually eat around 5:00 because we are so starving from smelling the intoxicating aroma all day. This family meal guarantees no complaints. In fact, my son William won't eat anything with tomatoes, but he loves this sauce. I tell him it's spaghetti sauce, not tomato sauce so he has no idea he's eating tomatoes.

1 lb piece of lean beef, such as eye of round
1 lb piece lean pork, such as loin
1 lb sweet sausage
3 T tomato paste
1/4 cup water
2 garlic cloves, minced
1 t sugar
3, 35 oz cans plum tomatoes
1 lb spaghetti, cooked and drained

- In a large stock pot over medium/high heat, add meat one at a time and brown on all sides, 5 minutes per piece. Once browned, remove from pot and drain on paper towels
- Combine tomato paste, water, garlic and sugar and add it to the pan. Cook for 2-3 minutes. Add tomatoes and their juice. Crush the tomatoes with a wooden spoon. Bring to a boil Add the meat, reduce heat, cover and simmer 2 hours until the meat is tender. Season with salt and pepper to taste
- Toss with spaghetti

Serves 4-6 with extra sauce

Summer Tomato Sauce

I do not have a green thumb. Our neighbors, David and Margie, have the most enviable vegetable garden. They cultivate their plants all spring in their basement and when the weather gets warm, they plant them outside. They usually have a few extra tomato plants and I'm always excited when they're offered to me. The only problem is that mine don't grow like theirs do. I came up with this recipe anticipating growing lots and lots of tomatoes. I started practicing with the ones sold at the farmer's market, which are excellent Jersey tomatoes. Fortunately, or unfortunately (I don't know which), I still buy my tomatoes as I'm still waiting for my own to grow.

5 lbs tomatoes
1 T sugar
1 T salt
1 head of garlic, separated but not peeled
4 T olive oil
1 cup (packed) basil, chopped
1 lb. spaghetti, cooked and drained

- Preheat oven to 200°
- Cut tomatoes in half, discard seeds and place cut side up on rimmed baking sheets lined with non stick aluminum foil. Place garlic around tomatoes, sprinkle with salt and sugar and drizzle with 2 T olive oil. Bake 3-4 hours
- Place tomatoes, garlic (squeezed out of skin) and juices in a food processor. Add basil, 2T olive oil and pulse to combine. Season with salt and pepper to taste
- Toss with spaghetti

Serves 4-6

Baked Stuffed Eggplant

When I was 16, I went to summer camp on a working farm in Iowa. We did everything from milking cows to feeding chickens to bailing hay. It was fun, hard work. This was a farm where they raised cattle to be turned into hamburger. I still have a hard time remembering their fate. The largest cow on the farm was named Amy. I was so upset. That poor cow with my name was living on borrowed time. I decided to become a vegetarian in sympathy. To my parent's shock, it lasted a whole year. My mother had to make two meals for dinner. One for the family and something vegetarian for me. This eggplant dish was one of my favorites.

1/2 cup flour
3 large eggs, beaten
3 cups bread crumbs (panko*)
2 cups (8 oz) Parmesan cheese, freshly grated
2 medium eggplants, sliced into

3 cups (12 oz) mozzarella cheese, grated
1 1/4 cup ricotta cheese
3/4 cup (packed) basil, chopped
32 oz can crushed tomatoes
6, 1/2"slices, 12 total

- Preheat oven to 350°
- Place flour, eggs and bread crumbs in three separate shallow bowls. Mix bread crumbs with 1 cup of the Parmesan cheese. Dredge each eggplant slice in flour, then egg, then bread crumb mixture. Arrange eggplant slices in a single layer on oiled, rimmed baking sheets. Bake 30 minutes until golden, turning after 15 minutes
- Meanwhile, mix 2 cups mozzarella, ricotta, basil and 1 cup Parmesan. Season with salt and pepper to taste.
- Place 1/3 of crushed tomatoes in the bottom of a 13x9" baking dish. Arrange 6 eggplant slices over tomatoes. Divide cheese mixture evenly over the eggplant, then place remaining eggplant over cheese mixture to make a sandwich. Spoon tomatoes over sandwiches. Sprinkle remaining mozzarella on top
- Bake uncovered, 30 minutes until bubbly

Serves 4-6

---

* Japanese breadcrumbs

Pesto

If you ask my kids if they know how to cook, they will proudly tell you that they can make pesto. Pesto is easy because it requires no cooking (except toasting pine nuts and the toasting does make a difference). The kids do the measuring. It all goes into the food processor and before they can start bickering, we have pesto. They love to eat it too. In the summer, when basil is plentiful, we'll make a bunch of batches and freeze them so we have pesto all winter long.

2 cup (packed) basil
1/2 cup Parmesan cheese, freshly grated
3 T pine nuts, toasted
1 garlic clove
2 T olive oil
1 lb penne, cooked and drained

- In a food processor, combine basil, Parmesan, pine nuts and garlic until smooth
- Slowly add olive oil in a steady stream. Season with salt and pepper to taste
- Toss with penne

Serves 4-6

Macaroni and Cheese

When my kids were much younger and developing their palates, I would spend hours in the kitchen making homemade macaroni and cheese. The kids would have a taste and declare in their tiny toddler voices that they wanted the kind in the box. I was shattered. I bought the box. Years later, my son, Jimmy asked me if I would ever make homemade macaroni and cheese again. I thought, here is my chance to prove that homemade is better than the box. So, I went to work but, I was smarter this time. So many recipes call for onions or breadcrumbs or nutmeg and cayenne pepper. Kids want it plain and simple, so that is how I made it. I know it was a success because the week I made it, they asked for it every night for dinner.

4 T unsalted butter
1/4 cup flour
2 cups whole milk
1/4 t Dijon mustard
4 cups (16oz) Cheddar cheese, grated
1 lb macaroni, cooked and drained

- Preheat oven to 400°
- In a large skillet over medium heat, melt butter. Add flour and cook 2 minutes stirring constantly until flour is absorbed. Wisk in milk and slowly bring to a simmer whisking constantly until slightly thickened, 3 minutes. Turn off heat and add mustard, 2 cups of cheese. Stir until cheese is melted. Season with salt and pepper to taste
- Add cooked macaroni and one cup of cheese and pour into a 13x9" baking dish. Sprinkle top with remaining cheese
- Cook until brown and bubbly, 25-30 minutes

Serves 6-8

Spaghetti with Fresh Clams

One night, Jim and I were having spaghetti with clams for dinner. The kids were asleep when we heard rustling at the top of the stairs. After a few minutes, we heard William timidly say, "Why are you eating shells?" Sure enough there was a plate in front of us piled high with discarded clam shells. It must have been quite a sight to for the little guy just exploring his epicurean boundaries. He was so cute with his curiosity, we let him try the "shells". He loved the dish so much that now when we go to restaurants he always asks if he can have spaghetti and clams.

1/2 cup olive oil
2 garlic cloves, minced
2 shallots, minced
3 lbs little neck clams in shells
1/4 cup + 2 T flat leaf parsley, chopped
1/2 cup white wine
1/4 cup fresh lemon juice
1 lb spaghetti, cooked and drained

- In a large pot over medium heat, sauté garlic and shallots in oil, 1 minute. Add clams and 1/4 cup parsley. Cook 2 minutes. Add wine and cook 2 more minutes. Add lemon juice. Cover and simmer until clams open, about 6 minutes (throw out unopened clams) Season with salt and pepper to taste
- Pour clam mixture over pasta (watch for sand that may have settled in the bottom of the pot). Sprinkle with remaining parsley

Serves 4-6

Orecchiette with Broccoli Rabe and Sausage

I don't know which I like more; this dish just after its made or the next day cold out of the container for lunch. The latter is definitely part of my motivation for making it, but it's satisfying both ways.

1 T olive oil
2 garlic clove, chopped
1 lb sweet Italian sausage casing removed
1 lb broccoli rabe, trimmed and chopped
1 cup broccoli rabe water
1 lb orecchiette pasta, cooked and drained
1/2 cup Parmesan cheese, freshly grated

- In a medium skillet over medium heat, cook sausage until cooked through and browned, 10 minutes. Drain on paper towels
- In another medium skillet, over low/medium heat toss garlic in oil to coat, 1 minute. Mix in sausage, turn off heat and set aside
- Meanwhile, in a large saucepan of water bring broccoli rabe to a boil and cook until tender, 8 minutes. Drain, reserving 1 cup cooking liquid
- Combine broccoli rabe and cooking liquid with sausage mixture. Season with salt and pepper to taste. Toss with orecchiette
- Sprinkle with Parmesan cheese

Serves 4-6

Paella

Making real Spanish paella is a complicated process. You need a special pan, fancy spices, and some time on your hands. Someday I would like to learn how to make paella that way. For now I make it this hassle free way. It's easy and delicious. I make it during the week all the time, but it would be a great one pot meal for a party too.

1/2 lb sausage (chorizo or anduille), sliced 1/4" thick
1 small onion, chopped
32 oz can (4 cups) chicken broth
1/2 t saffron threads
1 bay leaf
1 1/2 t fresh oregano, chopped
1 1/2 cups Arborio rice
1 lb shrimp, peeled and deveined
1 cup fresh peas (from about 1 lb shelled)
12 little neck clams in shells
1/4 cup white wine

- In a medium stockpot over medium heat cook sausage until browned, 5 minutes. Drain on paper towels. Add onion to the pan drippings and cook until soft, 3 minutes
- Add stock, saffron, bay leaf, oregano, and sausage. Turn heat to high and bring to a boil. Add rice, reduce heat to low, cover and simmer until rice has absorbed most of the liquid, 15 minutes. Add shrimp and peas and cook an additional 5 minutes
- In a medium saucepan cook clams in white wine until all of the clams have opened, about 5 minutes. Add clams and cooking liquid to rice mixture (watch for sand that may have settled in the bottom of the pot)
- Cover and remove from heat. Let rest 5 minutes before serving

Serves 4-6

Sesame Noodles with Chicken and Cucumber

I hate to admit this, but during the week, we do not have family dinners. It's really a matter of logistics. The kids have dinner around 6:00 and Jim and I eat closer to 8:00. Typically, while we're eating and the kids supposedly sleeping, William sheepishly comes down and sits with us as though it's his rite. At first, we were tough and kept shooing him back to bed. But, somehow our youngest child manages to manipulate his parents into eating a second dinner. Because he's so grateful to be sitting there, he enthusiastically tries everything. We told him he had a good palate and he loves to tell people that, even though we don't really think he understands what that means. One of his favorite late-night dishes are these sesame noodles.

1 lb chicken breasts
14 oz can chicken broth
1 large cucumber
3 T soy sauce
2 T sesame oil
1/2 cup tahini (sesame paste) or peanut butter
1 T seasoned rice vinegar
2 T sugar
dash of hot sauce
1 lb capellini, cooked and drained
3 scallions, trimmed and chopped

- In a medium saucepan, over medium/high heat poach chicken in broth, 10 minutes. Discard broth and shred chicken. Set aside
- Cut cucumber lengthwise, seed and thinly slice.
- Whisk together soy sauce, sesame oil, tahini, vinegar, sugar and hot sauce. Season with salt and pepper to taste (Thin with 1-2 tablespoons water if necessary)
- Toss with pasta, chicken and cucumber. Sprinkle scallions on top
- Serve at room temperature or cold

Serves 4-6

Greek Orzo Pasta Salad with Shrimp

My friends know that if they come to my house for lunch, there's a good chance they'll be eating orzo pasta salad. It's firmly entrenched in my repertory. So when my friend Jeanne asked me if I would make it for a family party she was having, I was flattered and wanted it to be perfect. Jeanne said the party was a great success, but apparently, in my insecurity, I made way too much. So around midnight with the party still going, Jeanne's brother Brian pulled it out of the refrigerator and accidentally dropped it. Instead of cleaning it up, he grabbed a fork, sat on the kitchen floor (Jeanne's house is spotless) and enjoyed the leftovers. I consider that the best compliment of all.

1 lb orzo pasta
2 T olive oil
2 T fresh lemon juice
1 T red wine vinegar
1 large tomato, seeded and chopped
3 scallions, trimmed and chopped

4 oz container feta cheese crumbled
1 lb jumbo shrimp, cooked with tail off
1 cup kalamata olives, pitted and cut in half
1/2 cup fresh dill, chopped

- In a medium stock pot, cook pasta, 8 minutes. Rinse in cold water and toss with 1 tablespoon olive oil. Set aside
- In a small bowl whisk lemon juice, olive oil, and vinegar. Season with salt and pepper to taste. Set aside
- In a large serving bowl, combine orzo with tomato, scallions, feta, shrimp and olives. Toss with vinaigrette. Sprinkle dill on top and toss again

Serves 4-6

<u>Meat</u>

Beef Burgundy

When I first started entertaining, my repertory was limited to this recipe. It cannot be ruined. Just throw it all in a pot, cook for a few hours and, voila!, you are ready for your dinner party. You can even make it the day before or early in the morning and re-heat it when you are ready to serve. Serve it over noodles with a green salad and you're set.

2 lbs lean beef, cubed
1/2 cup flour
salt and pepper
10 3/4 oz can tomato soup
10 1/4 oz can onion soup
1/2 cup half and half
1/2 cup red wine
8 oz package mushrooms, sliced
1 lb egg noodles, cooked and drained

- Preheat oven to 300º
- Place flour, salt and pepper in a bowl. Dredge beef in flour mixture and place in a Dutch oven. Add soups, undiluted
- Bake covered 2 1/2 hours (add a water or broth if meat gets dry). Add half and half, wine and mushrooms and cook for 30 minutes more until beef is fork tender
- Serve over egg noodles.

Serves 4-6

Boeuf Bourguignon

If snow is in the forecast, Jim has one dinner request: Boeuf Bourguignon. There's nothing better on a snowy night, preferably on the weekend (so you can sleep late the next day) with a plate of this hearty country French beef stew and a glass of Merlot. I don't like to pair this dish with noodles or anything for that matter except some crusty French bread to sop up the gravy.

2 lbs lean beef, cubed
marinade:
1 bottle red wine
2 celery stalks, chopped
2 large carrots, peeled and chopped
2 onions, chopped
1 bulb garlic, unpeeled and
cut horizontally
2 bay leaves
pinch thyme
1 T whole black peppercorns

sauce:
2 T unsalted butter
2 T olive oil
8 oz pancetta, diced
4 shallots, chopped
3 T Dijon mustard

- In a large bowl, combine beef with marinade and refrigerate overnight
- Drain beef reserving marinade liquid. Remove peppercorns, onions and garlic from marinade and discard. Separate vegetables from meat. Dry meat on paper towels
- In a large stockpot, over high heat, sear the beef in butter and oil. Remove and add pancetta. Cook for 3-4 minutes. Remove pancetta, reduce heat to medium, add shallots and cook until soft. Add marinated vegetables, pancetta, beef and mustard. Cook 3-4 minutes. Add marinade. Bring to a boil, reduce to a simmer, cover and cook 2 hours. The sauce should be thick and the meat fork tender (add water or broth if meat gets too dry)

Serves 4-6

Grilled, Marinated Flank Steak (Good Marinade for Beef)

This is my sister-in-law Kelley's recipe. It's such a favorite in the Currie family, we all know it by heart. It's perfect for a summer barbecue and the leftovers make a great steak sandwich the next day.

2 flank steaks (1-1 1/2 lbs each)
marinade:
3 cloves garlic, minced
3 T olive oil
1/2 cup tomato juice
1/2 cup fresh lime juice (about 2)
1/2 cup soy sauce
1/2 cup packed light brown sugar
1 t ground pepper

- In a small bowl mix all marinade ingredients
- Pour marinade over meat turning to coat, cover and refrigerate overnight turning occasionally
- Heat grill to medium/high. Remove steak from marinade and grill about 10 minutes on each side
- Pour remaining marinade in a small saucepan and bring to a boil, uncovered. Then, reduce to a simmer and continue cooking for 10 minutes
- Remove steak from grill, rest 10 minutes and slice
- Serve with sauce

Serves 4-6

Grilled, Marinated London broil (Really Good Marinade for Beef)

While working on a cookbook for a local organization, I came across this recipe. As a committee member, we tested hundreds of recipes. I kept putting this one on the bottom of my pile because I didn't want to try another beef marinade since I love my sister-in-law Kelley's so much. Well, I finally did try it and it is so amazing. There is room in the culinary world for more than one beef marinade.

1 London broil (2-2 1/2 lbs)
marinade:
1/2 cup red wine
1/4 cup extra virgin olive oil
1/4 cup Dijon mustard
2 T fresh rosemary, chopped
6 garlic cloves, minced
1/2 t freshly ground pepper
salt to taste

- In a food processor, combine all marinade ingredients until smooth
- Pour marinade over meat, turning to coat. Cover and refrigerate overnight turning occasionally
- Heat grill to medium/high. Remove steak from marinade and grill about 15 minutes per side. Discard marinade
- Remove from grill, let rest 10 minutes and slice

Serves 4-6

Flank Steak with Apple Sausage Stuffing

This is my friend Tracy's recipe. I was at her house one day several years ago dropping off a carpool of kids and she was preparing this for dinner. Without even trying it, I had to have the recipe. It's such a flavorful combination and very tasty on a cold winter night.

1 lb sweet Italian sausage, casing removed
1 medium onion, chopped
1 granny smith apple, peeled, seeded, and chopped
1 flank steak, butterflied (1-1 1/2 lbs)
1 large egg
1/2 cup bread crumbs (fresh)
1/3 cup Madeira wine
1/2 cup barbecue sauce

- In large skillet over medium/high heat, cook sausage until no longer pink, 10 minutes. Drain. Add onions and apples and cook until soft and nicely combined with sausage, 5 minutes. Set aside to cool
- Meanwhile pound each flank steak to tenderize. Cover and set aside
- Add egg, bread crumbs and wine to cooled sausage mixture
- Preheat oven to 350°
- Spread 1 cup of stuffing on 1 flank steak and roll lengthwise with the grain like a jelly roll. Place seam side down in 13x9" baking dish. Repeat with the other flank steak. Brush both steaks with barbecue sauce reserving any extra. Spread extra stuffing around steaks
- Bake 1 hour, basting every 10 minutes.
- Let steaks rest 10 minutes before slicing

Serves 4-6

Sloppy Joes

My mom used to make my brothers and me sloppy joes when I was growing up. She's an inspiring cook, but back in the 70's, it seemed that everything came out of a can, which was my first introduction to this ground beef stew on a bun. I knew my kids would like it, so I bought a can, read the ingredients and re-created a homemade version. It is now a great staple in our household and not much harder to make than the canned version but, much, much better.

1 lb lean ground beef
1 small onion, chopped
1 t Dijon mustard
1 t Worcestershire sauce
1 t sugar
1 t white wine vinegar

1/2 cup ketchup
1/2 t salt
1 celery stalk, chopped
4 hamburger buns

- In a medium skillet over medium/high heat brown meat, 10 minutes. Drain excess fat. In the same skillet, add onion, mustard, Worcestershire, vinegar, ketchup, salt, and celery. Reduce heat to low, cover and cook 15 minutes, stirring occasionally (add water if mixture gets too dry)
- Ladle meat evenly on bottom half of each hamburger bun. Place top bun over sloppy joe

Serves 4

Untraditional Meat Loaf

We all love meat loaf in our family, and there are so many ways to make it. I was getting tired of traditional meatloaf with ketchup or tomato sauce, and I wanted to do something totally different. Since mustard goes great on a hamburger, I thought it could be an interesting ingredient in meatloaf. The dill takes it in an unusual direction as a substitution for thyme or oregano, which you would use in a more traditional version.

3/4 cup beef broth
1/2 cup old fashioned oats
1 1/2 lbs meat loaf mix
(equal parts ground beef, pork and veal)
1 small onion, chopped
1/2 cup chopped fresh dill
3 T grainy mustard

1/2 t salt
1/2 t pepper
1 large egg

- Preheat oven to 400°
- In a medium bowl, mix broth with oats and soak 5 minutes. Add remaining ingredients to oat mixture. Mix well and form into one or two loaves (if you're not cooking for 4-6, you can freeze one). Place in a foil lined, rimmed baking sheet
- Bake 1 hour for one loaf and 50 minutes for two until browned and cooked through. Remove and drain on paper towels
- Cool 10-15 minutes, then transfer to a serving platter

Serves 4-6

Nanny's Brisket

My mother's mother, Nanny, was a tremendous influence on me. She was an incredible Jewish cook, making all the traditional favorites like matzo ball soup, chopped liver and brisket. Before she passed away, she wrote all of her recipes down and gave them to me. They're a treasure. For years it drove me crazy trying to figure out proper measurements and serving sizes. I began to realize that these recipes were passed down from generation to generation and serving size...well...does it really matter? This is my interpretation of my Nanny's brisket, measurements and all and it tastes exactly the way I remember it.

1 first cut brisket (3-3 1/2 lbs))
l large onion, chopped
2 T olive oil
10 3/4 oz can cream of mushroom soup
14 oz can crushed tomatoes
1/2 cup red wine

- In a large skillet over medium heat sauté onion in oil until soft, 5 minutes. Remove onion and place in a Dutch oven. Set aside
- In the same skillet, turn heat to high, season brisket with salt and pepper and brown on both sides, 2 minutes per side. Place on top of onions in the Dutch oven. Pour mushroom soup (undiluted) and tomatoes (with juice) over brisket. Cover and simmer over low heat for 2 hours, turning every 1/2 hour (Add water or broth if brisket becomes too dry). Add wine and cook another 1/2 hour until fork tender
- Let rest 10 minutes before slicing

Serves 6-8

Barbecued Brisket

This is a recipe that I came across several years ago. I cannot remember its origins, but it's a favorite none-the-less. It's very different from my Nanny's, yet still has incredibly tender results due to the sweet and savory sauce. This brisket is a great Sunday night winter dish.

1 fist cut brisket (3-3 1/2 lbs)
32 oz can (4 cups) beef broth
1 medium onion, chopped
1 t dry mustard
1/3 cup apple cider vinegar
1 T Worcestershire sauce
1/4 cup chili sauce
1/4 cup packed light brown sugar

2 t salt
dash hot sauce

- In a large skillet over medium heat sauté onion in oil until soft, 5 minutes. Remove onion and place in a Dutch oven. Set aside
- In the same skillet, turn heat to high, season brisket with salt and pepper and brown on both sides, 2 minutes per side. Place on top of onions in the Dutch oven. Pour beef broth over brisket. Bring to a boil, cover and reduce heat to low. Simmer 1 1/2 hours (add water or broth if brisket becomes too dry)
- Combine mustard, vinegar, Worcestershire, chili sauce and brown sugar. Pour over brisket. Cook one more hour until fork tender
- Let rest 10 minutes before slicing

Serves 6-8

<u>Moussaka</u>

When I was living in New York City after college, my friends and I never tired of having new culinary adventures. One of our favorite dining experiences was Greek food in Astoria, Queens. Just a subway ride away, there were dozens of authentic Greek restaurants in this little neighborhood. We shared everything, not wanting to miss a flavor. My favorite was moussaka, a traditional ground lamb dish with a béchamel sauce, but it seemed complicated to make. Then, several years ago, I came across a lighter version with ground beef and a topping combining feta and ricotta cheeses. I can't say it's authentic, but it's really good and my kids like it too!

1 large eggplant (2-2 1/2 lbs), peeled and cut into 1" cubes
4 T olive oil
1/2 T salt
1/2 t pepper
2 small onions, chopped
2 garlic cloves, minced
1 lb lean ground beef
28 oz can whole tomatoes, drained

2 t tomato paste
1/2 cup flat leaf parsley, chopped
2 T fresh oregano
1 t cinnamon
9 oz container ricotta cheese
4 oz container feta cheese, crumbled
1 large egg

- Preheat oven to 400°
- Place eggplant on a baking sheet and toss with 3 tablespoons olive oil, salt and pepper. Bake until soft and golden, 30 minutes. Transfer to a 13x9" baking dish. Set aside
- In a medium skillet, over medium heat, sauté onions and garlic in remaining oil until soft, 5 minutes. Add beef and cook until meat is browned, 8-10 minutes. Add tomatoes (crush with a wooden spoon), tomato paste, parsley, oregano and cinnamon and cook 15 more minutes. Season with salt and pepper to taste. Spread over eggplant. Set aside
- In a small bowl, combine ricotta, feta and egg. Pour mixture over meat
- Bake until top is lightly browned, 15 minutes

Serves 4-6

Pork Tenderloin with Molasses Barbecue Sauce

Pork tenderloin is a lean and delicious cut of meat. I love this combination of mustard and molasses. It gives the pork a little kick. You can serve this warm or at room temperature, sliced or in a sandwich, which Makesit great for a party.

1/2 cup unsulphured molasses
1 T grainy Dijon mustard
1/2 t dry mustard
1/2 t ground ginger
juice and zest of 1 lemon
2 pork tenderloins (2-2 1/2lbs)

- In a small bowl combine molasses, mustards, ginger, lemon juice and zest. Place pork in a 13x9" baking dish. Sprinkle with salt and pepper and coat with half of the molasses mixture. Chill 2 hours to overnight
- Heat grill to medium/high. Sear tenderloin 2-3 minutes per side
- Brush on remaining molasses mixture. Cook covered, 15 minutes, basting often
- Let pork rest 10 minutes before slicing

Serves 4-6

Nanny's Baby Back Ribs

My son Jimmy loves ribs. If a restaurant has ribs on the menu, Jimmy always orders them. Remembering the taste of my grandmother's version, I took to her treasure of recipes to find her take on this delicious dish. The easiest thing about it is that they're cooked in the oven, so they can be made any time. If you do want that char-grilled look and flavor, throw them on the grill heated to medium/high heat for 10 minutes after they've cooked in the oven 1 1/2 hours.

1/2 cup packed light brown sugar
2 T Worcestershire sauce
14 oz can tomato puree
1 t salt

1 T paprika
1 T chili powder
1/2 T cumin
5 lbs baby back pork ribs

- In a small bowl, whisk together brown sugar, Worcestershire, tomato puree, salt, paprika, chili powder and cumin
- Place ribs, in a rimmed baking sheet and pour marinade over. Covered and chill 2 hours to overnight, turning occasionally
- Preheat oven to 325º
- Line a broiler pan with non-stick aluminum foil and place ribs rounded side up. Reserve marinade for basting
- Bake 1 3/4-2 hours, basting every 20-30 minutes until meat is fork tender (Do not use any more marinade the last 20 minutes of cooking). Discard leftover marinade
- Let rest 10 minutes before serving

Serves 4-6

Poultry

Lemon Chicken Cutlets

There's a famous restaurant in New York City that's nearly impossible to get into. It's very small and has a regular, celebrity clientele, so chances are, us common folk will never get to go there. They've published a cookbook, however, which I love. The lemon chicken is a great dish, but sometimes I find that food cooked in a restaurant needs to be adapted for home cooking. It's just a personal thing, but I prefer using as little oil or butter as possible because I've never found all that extra fat to be a critical ingredient in a recipe. So, I took this recipe and modified it. It has an unbelievable lemony flavor, which is really the essence, but has home-style appeal, just the way I like it.

4 large boneless, skinless chicken breasts (about 2 lbs), butterflied
1 large egg
1 cup bread crumbs (panko*)
3 T flat leaf parsley, chopped
1/2 t paprika
1/2 t salt

1/2 t pepper
2 T unsalted butter
1/4 cup olive oil + 2 T
1/2 cup fresh lemon juice (3-4 lemons)
1/2 t red wine vinegar
1 garlic clove, minced

- Cut each chicken breast in half, then, pound between two pieces of plastic wrap until 1/2" thick (There should be 8 pieces)
- Meanwhile, in a small bowl, whisk egg with 1 tablespoon water. In another small bowl, combine bread crumbs, 1 tablespoon parsley, paprika, salt and pepper. Dredge chicken in egg, then bread crumb mixture
- In a large skillet over medium/high heat, combine 1 tablespoon butter and 1 tablespoon olive oil. Place chicken, 4 pieces at a time, in skillet and cook 3 minutes on each side until lightly browned. Remove and transfer to a 13x9" baking dish. Repeat with remaining butter, oil and chicken
- Preheat broiler

---

* Japanese breadcrumbs

- In a small bowl, combine lemon juice, 1/4 cup olive oil, vinegar and garlic. Season with salt and pepper to taste. Pour over chicken and broil 10 minutes until sauce is bubbly and chicken is crispy. Sprinkle with 2 tablespoons parsley and serve

Serves 4-6

Chicken and Broccoli Divan

After I graduated from college, I set my sights on working in New York City. Being a Philadelphia girl, I didn't have a lot of connections to finding a job or a place to live. By day, I pounded the pavement. By night, I was a guest to any friend who would let me crash on their couch. One week I stayed with my friend Nancy at her sister's apartment. Penny was married with kids and lived in a beautiful building in midtown. It was heavenly. She made us breakfast and dinner every day. One of my favorite meals was chicken divan. I had never had it, but it was a far cry from pizza. In the years following, I tried to find the recipe, but was unsuccessful. So, I made it up. I don't know if this is traditional chicken divan, but I think it's pretty good.

2 lbs boneless, skinless chicken breasts
2, 14 oz cans chicken broth
4 T (1/2 stick) unsalted butter
1 small onion, chopped
2 garlic cloves, minced
1/2 t dry mustard

4 T Dijon mustard
2 cups bread crumbs (panko*)
1 cup (4oz) Parmesan cheese freshly grated
1 bunch broccoli trimmed, and chopped
1 cup half and half

- In a medium saucepan over medium/high heat poach chicken in the broth, 10 minutes. Drain (discarding broth), cool and cut into 1 1/2" pieces. Set aside
- In a large skillet over medium heat, sauté onion and garlic in butter until soft, 5 minutes. Whisk in dry mustard and 2 tablespoons Dijon mustard. Add bread crumbs and sauté until crisp and golden, 5 minutes, stirring often. Turn off heat and add 3/4 cup Parmesan. Season with salt and pepper to taste. Set aside
- In a large saucepan of water, cook broccoli until crisp tender, 5 minutes. Drain, set aside
- Preheat oven to 350°

---

* Japanese breadcrumbs

- Place broccoli and chicken in a large bowl. Add half and half, 2 tablespoons Dijon mustard and 1/4 cup Parmesan. Toss to coat. Pour in a 13x9" baking dish. Sprinkle topping over chicken mixture
- Bake 30 minutes until bubbly

Serves 6-8

"Fancy" Chicken Nuggets

Recently, my daughter Catie was at her friend Bailey's house for dinner. They were served chicken nuggets. Catie, eating contentedly said, "These are good, but you know, my mom Makes "fancy" chicken nuggets". Later, Bailey's mom called and said "What in the world are "fancy" chicken nuggets?" I had no idea, but I suspected they were the homemade ones that I make all the time. I usually make a big batch and freeze them cooked. I heat up as many as I need and the kids love them. They also make a great hors d'oeuvre.

1 cup buttermilk
1 cup bread crumbs (panko*)
1 cup (4 oz) Parmesan cheese, freshly grated
2 lbs chicken breasts cut into 1 1/2" pieces

- Preheat oven to 400°
- Place buttermilk in a small bowl. In another small bowl, mix bread crumbs and Parmesan cheese. Dredge chicken, a few pieces at a time, in buttermilk, then bread crumb/Parmesan mixture. Place on a greased baking sheet
- Bake 30 minutes until chicken is golden
- Serve immediately or freeze

Serves 4-6

---

* Japanese breadcrumbs

Chicken and Spinach Braciole

My friend Becky had a very special dinner party one fall. She made her grandmothers gravy. This gravy has a lot of history. It's a traditional Italian spaghetti sauce that takes days to make and includes meatballs, sausage, chicken wings and braciole. It was such an incredible meal that when it was over, I could barely get out of my chair. The braciole, in particular, was my favorite; thin slices of beef rolled up cigar-style with Parmesan and parsley inside. A classic Italian dish, Becky sautéed them, them cooked them further in the sauce. Days later I was still dreaming of that braciole, so I decided to create my own recipe. This chicken version is not quite the same, but it's delicious and has its own personality even if it was created from an old classic.

4 large boneless, skinless chicken
breasts (about 2 lbs), butterflied
5 T olive oil
3 T unsalted butter
2 garlic cloves, minced
1 small onion, chopped
10 oz bag baby spinach
1 1/2 cups bread crumbs (fresh)
1/2 cup whole milk
1/3 cup (1 1/2 oz) Parmesan cheese, freshly grated
6 oz package mushrooms, chopped
1 T flour
1 cup white wine

- Preheat oven to 350°
- Cut each chicken breast in half, then pound between plastic wrap until 1/4" thick. (there should be 8 pieces) Season with salt and pepper and set aside
- In a large skillet over medium heat, sauté garlic and onion in 1 tablespoon butter and 1 tablespoon oil until soft, 5 minutes. Add spinach and toss until wilted, 1 minute. Remove from heat and set aside
- In a medium bowl, combine bread crumbs with milk and add to spinach mixture. Then, add Parmesan and mix thoroughly.

Divide evenly on top of the chicken. Roll up each piece like a cigar and tie with kitchen string or secure with toothpicks

- In a large skillet over medium/high heat, sauté 4 braciole's in 2 tablespoons oil until chicken is brown on all sides, 8 minutes. Transfer to a 13x9" baking dish. Repeat with remaining oil and braciole
- In same skillet, sauté mushrooms in 2 tablespoons butter until they release their juices, 8 minutes. Add flour and whisk until absorbed, 1 minute. Whisk in wine, cook 1 minute to reduce and thicken sauce. Season with salt and pepper to taste. Pour sauce over chicken. Bake covered for 20 minutes

Serves 4-6

Moroccan Chicken

When I lived in New York City, my roommate Mary's boyfriend was from Morocco. Mary was a great cook and always interested in expanding her repertory. I loved coming home to the exotic smell of Moroccan food cooking in the kitchen. Occasionally, I peeked over her shoulder and I actually learned a bit. The dish that I remember most is Moroccan chicken, which I have adapted, and make all the time now. I love the combination of the cumin and cinnamon with the honey and green olives. It is completely different from anything I make and I look forward to it every time.

4 large boneless, skinless chicken breasts (about 2 lbs) butterflied
1/4 cup flour + salt and pepper
3 T olive oil
1 medium onion, chopped
juice and zest of 1 lemon
1 1/2 t cumin
1/2 t paprika
1/2 t cinnamon

14 oz can chicken broth
1/2 cup green olives, pitted and sliced
1 T honey
1/4 cup cilantro, chopped
15 oz can garbanzo beans, drained

- Cut each chicken breast in half, then pound between plastic wrap until 1/2" thick (there should be 8 pieces).
- In a small bowl, combine flour, salt and pepper. Dredge chicken in flour and tap off excess
- Heat 1 tablespoon oil in a large skillet over medium/high heat. Add chicken, 4 pieces at a time and cook 3 minutes on each side until lightly browned. Remove and set aside. Repeat with oil and remaining chicken
- In same skillet over medium heat, sauté onion in 1 tablespoon oil until soft, 5 minutes. Add lemon zest and juice, cumin, paprika, cinnamon, broth and olives and simmer 1 minute
- Return chicken to skillet. Bring to a boil over medium heat. Simmer 8-10 minutes, turning chicken once. Transfer chicken to a serving platter. Add honey, cilantro and beans to sauce and cook 2 more minutes to heat through

- Pour over chicken and serve

Serves 4- 6

Chicken Marsala

One of the challenges of raising kids is the often unbearable experience of dining out. There are basically two types of restaurants. The kid friendly version: great, but no fun for us parents and face it, we're paying. Then there's the "nice" restaurant. The adult part of you appreciates the ambience and the food, but the parent in you panics because there's no kid's menu. A restaurant that doesn't have a kid's menu is an unspoken rule for no kids. Luckily for us there's a restaurant in our town that creates a harmonious balance. It's good old fashioned Italian food with a wine list. The kids love the spaghetti and meatballs and we love the chicken marsala. In fact, we love it so much, I started making my own version at home.

4 large boneless, skinless chicken breasts (about 2 lbs), butterflied
1/4 cup flour + 1T
2 t salt
1 t pepper
2 T olive oil
4 T (1/2 stick) unsalted butter
8 oz package mushrooms, sliced

1 T flour
1 cup Marsala wine
1 garlic clove, minced
juice of 1 lemon
2 T flat leaf parsley, chopped

- Cut each chicken breast in half, then pound between plastic wrap until 1/2" thick. (there should be 8 pieces)
- In a small bowl, combine flour, salt, and pepper. Dredge chicken and tap off excess
- Heat 1 tablespoon oil in a large skillet over medium/high heat. Add chicken, four pieces at a time and cook 3 minutes on each side until lightly browned. Remove and set aside. Repeat with oil and remaining chicken
- In same skillet, over medium heat sauté mushrooms and garlic in 2 tablespoons butter until mushrooms release their liquid, 8 minutes. Add 1 tablespoon flour and whisk until absorbed, 1 minute. Remove from heat. Add Marsala and return to heat. Add lemon juice and 2 tablespoons butter. Whisk until thickened, 2 minutes. Season with salt and pepper to taste

- Pour sauce over chicken, sprinkle with parsley

Serves 4-6

Turkey Meatloaf

This recipe is from my friend Christina's repertory. It's a great weeknight dinner that our whole family loves, even picky children. A great option is to make it into two loaves and freeze one for another time.

1 T olive oil
2 shallots, minced
1/2 green pepper, seeded
and chopped
2 celery stalks, chopped
2 garlic cloves, minced
2 lbs ground turkey

8 oz can tomato sauce
1 cup bread crumbs (fresh)
2 large eggs
2 t salt

- Preheat oven to 375°
- In a large skillet over medium heat, sauté shallots, peppers, celery and garlic in oil until soft, 8 minutes.
- In a large bowl, combine turkey, tomato sauce, bread crumbs, and eggs. Mix in sautéed vegetables
- Form into one or two loaves (If you're not cooking for 4-6, you can freeze one)
- Place on a rimmed baking sheet lined with non-stick aluminum foil and bake 1 hour for one loaf and 50 minutes for two

Serves 4-6

Turkey Meatloaf Florentine

I grew up with two brothers. We were all close, but they were closer. When I started dating Jim, his family invited me to join them on a ski trip. There were three bedrooms in the rented chalet: One for his parents, one for Jim and his brother, and one for his sister and me (hey, we were just dating and it was a family vacation). Well, Christy and I had such a great time. She was still in college so we talked all night about college life and my advertising job in New York City (she ended up in the same profession). We were sisters from the beginning, and I couldn't believe how lucky I was. Many years later, Christy and I are still very close. Since she got married, she has developed a real appreciation for cooking. This is one of her favorites which I make all the time.

1 T unsalted butter
1 T olive oil
1 medium onion, chopped
6 oz package of mushrooms, sliced
10 oz package frozen, chopped
spinach drained of all liquid
1/4 cup (1 oz) Parmesan cheese,
freshly grated
1/2 cup (2 oz) mozzarella cheese,
grated

1 lb ground turkey
1 large egg white
lightly beaten
3/4 cups old fashioned oats
1/2 cup whole milk
2 T Italian seasoning
1/2 t garlic powder
1/2 t onion powder
2 T tomato paste

- Preheat oven to 375°
- In a medium skillet, over medium heat sauté mushrooms and onions in butter and oil until mushrooms release their liquid and onions are soft, 8 minutes. Remove from heat and add spinach and both cheeses. Set aside
- In a medium bowl combine turkey, egg white, oats, milk, Italian seasoning, garlic and onion powders. Season with salt and pepper
- On a rimmed baking sheet fitted with non-stick aluminum foil, place 2/3 of the turkey mixture in a rectangle. Put the spinach mixture on top leaving 1" border of turkey. Place the remaining turkey on top, covering the spinach. Pinch the sides and mold it to

look like a loaf. Spread the tomato paste all over the top and bake
1 hour
* Let rest 10 minutes before slicing

Serves 4-6

Chicken Pot Pie

Every Saturday night when I was growing up, my parents went out for the evening and our special treat was a TV dinner. My brothers went for the one that came with the half baked, tasteless desert. I liked chicken pot pie. Actually, I liked the idea of the chicken pot pie, but I always wished there were different vegetables. So, now I make my own just the way I like it. I use white meat chicken, carrots, celery, and broccoli. No peas — Yea!

1 1/2 lbs boneless, skinless chicken breasts, cubed
14 oz can chicken broth
1 1/2 T canola oil
1 medium onion, chopped
3 carrots, peeled and chopped
2 celery stalks, chopped
1 head of broccoli, trimmed and chopped

4 T unsalted butter
1/2 cup flour
1 1/2 cups whole milk
1/2 t thyme
1 sheet puff pastry
(half a 17.3 oz box)

- Preheat oven to 400°
- In a medium saucepan poach chicken in broth, 10 minutes. Transfer chicken to a 13x9" baking dish and broth to a small bowl.
- In a large skillet, over medium heat, sauté onion, carrots, broccoli and celery in oil until soft, 15 minute. Add cooked vegetables to chicken. Set aside
- In a medium saucepan, melt butter. Whisk in flour and cook for 1 minute. Whisk in reserved chicken broth, milk, accumulated chicken juices and thyme. Bring to a boil, and then reduce to a simmer until sauce thickens, 1 minute. Season with salt and pepper to taste. Pour sauce over chicken-vegetable mixture
- Roll out puff pastry to the size of the dish and place on top
- Bake 30 minutes until top is puffed and golden

Serves 6-8

Enchilada Pie (Mexican Lasagna)

I learned of this recipe several years ago when I was walking with my friend Maria. Her sister Elizabeth had joined us for our morning routine and was surprised to learn that we only talked about one thing; food. I'm sure it was so boring for her listening to us going on and on about recipes, menu planning and ingredients. A couple of miles into our walk she spoke, "I have a great recipe. It's called Enchilada Pie". I listened and it sounded great. I went right to the store, bought the ingredients and made it that night. Even the kids loved the pie and it freezes well. It's now one of our regular weeknight dinners.

14 oz can chicken broth
1/2-3/4 lb boneless, skinless chicken breast
1 T canola oil
1 medium onion, chopped
24 oz can enchilada sauce
12, 6" corn tortillas
8 oz container sour cream
8 oz package Monterey Jack cheese, shredded

- In a medium saucepan, poach chicken in chicken broth, 10 minutes. Cool and shred chicken, reserving broth
- Preheat oven to 350°
- In a medium skillet, over medium heat, sauté onion in oil until soft, 5 minutes. Add shredded chicken to onions along with 1/2 cup cooking broth and 1/2 cup sour cream. Stir over low heat until combined.
- Place a thin layer of enchilada sauce in an 8" square baking dish, then cover with 4 tortillas, 1/3 chicken mixture, 2 tablespoons sour cream, and 1/3 of cheese. Continue in this order two more times and finish with remaining cheese on top
- Bake for 30 minutes until brown and bubbly

Serves 4-6

Turkey Tetrazzini

When we had our first Thanksgiving at home, I was so excited I bought a gigantic turkey. It barely fit in the oven, but it was delicious. Afterwards, there were way too many leftovers. I know this is a common situation on Thanksgiving, but I never had to deal with it before. My neighbor, Mary Ann came to my rescue with this recipe. It's almost just as good as the freshly roasted turkey, and I'm already looking forward to having leftovers next year.

1/2 cup (1 stick) unsalted butter
1 medium onion, chopped
6 oz package of mushrooms, sliced
1/2 cup flour
2 cups chicken broth
2 cups half and half
6 cups cooked turkey, cubed
1 cup (4 oz) Parmesan cheese, freshly grated

1 cup (4 oz) Swiss cheese, grated
1 lb thin spaghetti
1 cup bread crumbs (panko*)

- Preheat oven to 350°
- Cook pasta in boiling water for 5 minutes (will not be cooked through). Drain and set aside
- In a large saucepan over medium heat, sauté onion and mushrooms in butter until mushrooms have released their liquid and onion is soft, 8 minutes. Add flour and stir until absorbed, 2 minutes. Add chicken broth and half and half. Bring to a boil. Reduce and simmer until the sauce thickens. Add turkey and cheeses and stir until cheeses are melted. Toss with pasta
- Place in a 13x9" baking dish
- Top with bread crumbs. Bake 30 minutes until bubbly

Serves 6-8

---

* Japanese breadcrumbs

Fish and Seafood

Grilled Salmon with Cucumber Sauce

This dish is not about the salmon. It's great on the grill, but as you can see, there's nothing to it. The cucumber sauce is an amazing accompaniment to salmon whether it's grilled, poached, or roasted, as long as it is simply cooked.

2 lb salmon fillet whole or cut into fillets
salt and pepper

Cucumber Sauce:
1 cup plain low fat yogurt
1 cup sour cream
1 medium cucumber, peeled, seeded and chopped
2 scallions, trimmed and chopped
1/4 cup fresh mint, chopped
1/4 cup fresh dill, chopped

- Cucumber sauce: place yogurt in a colander lined with paper towels fitted over a bowl. Let drain 1 hour (yogurt will reduce by half). In a small bowl, combine yogurt with sour cream, cucumber, scallions, mint and dill. Season with salt and pepper to taste.
- Spray grill with non-stick spray. Heat on medium/high. Sprinkle salmon with salt and pepper and grill 7 minutes on each side
- Serve with cucumber sauce

Serves 4 with extra cucumber sauce

Cold Poached Salmon

At least once every summer there's a heat wave that seems to never end. The weatherman calls it the three H's: hazy, hot and humid, and the last thing I feel like doing is cooking. When I do, I turn to poached salmon. Not only is it easy with minimal ingredients, it's served cold, which is really all you want on a hot summer day. Serve with cucumber sauce.

2 lb salmon fillet,
whole or cut into 4 fillets
1/3 cup water
1/3 cup white wine
1 shallot, minced

4 parsley sprigs
1 fresh thyme sprig

- In a large skillet over high heat, bring water, wine, shallot, parsley and thyme to a boil. Place salmon fillet(s) skin side down in skillet. Sprinkle with salt and pepper. Cover skillet and simmer over medium/low heat until salmon is barely opaque in center, 10 minutes
- Remove from heat, let rest covered 5 more minutes
- Transfer to a serving platter and chill. Discard wine mixture
- Serve with lemon wedges and cucumber sauce (page 149)

Serves 4

Marinated, Roasted Salmon

This is another weekday winner, but you could easily serve it at a dinner party. I like the marinade because there's no added fat. The salmon itself has enough (healthy fat!), so the marinade simply enhances the flavor. A word of caution: do not over marinate or you not only loose the delicate flavor of the fish, but the texture will get mealy. You can also easily grill the fish as an alternative to roasting. Just follow the "grilled salmon" directions.

1/3 cup white wine
1/3 cup fresh orange juice
1/3 cup soy sauce
2 lb salmon fillet whole or cut into 4 fillets

- Mix wine, juice and soy sauce in a rimmed baking dish. Add salmon flesh side down, turning to coat. Cover and chill 2 hours, turning after 1 hour
- Preheat oven to 450°
- Place salmon skin side down on rimmed baking sheet lined with non-stick aluminum foil. Sprinkle with salt and pepper. Roast 14 minutes until fish is cooked through
- Place reserved marinade in a small saucepan, bring to a boil and cook until reduced by half, 10 minutes. Drizzle over salmon

Serves 4

Salmon with Mustard-Crumb Crust

This is probably my all time favorite salmon recipe. I love its simplicity as a weeknight dinner but it's just as fabulous for entertaining. I came up with this recipe one night when I bought salmon but needed a new idea. I was trying to re-create all those crusted fish dishes that restaurants serve and I happened to have these ingredients in the pantry. Here's a tip for fresh bread crumbs. Whenever there's leftover bread (French, Italian, or white), I pulse it in a food processor to make bread crumbs. I store my fresh bread crumbs in the freezer and measure the exact amount whenever I need it. I don't like the idea of using stale bread. If you want your bread crumbs dry, just spread them out on a baking sheet and toast in a 300° oven for about 15 minutes.

2 1/2 T white wine vinegar
2 T sugar
2 T Dijon mustard
1 1/2 t dry mustard
1/4 cup canola oil

2 lb salmon fillet whole
or cut into 4 fillets
1 t dried thyme
salt and pepper
1 cup bread crumbs (fresh)

- Preheat oven to 375°
- In a food processor combine vinegar, sugar and both mustards. Slowly drizzle in oil and blend until sauce forms. Set aside
- Arrange salmon skin side down on a 13x9" baking dish. Season with thyme, salt and pepper. Spread sauce over salmon, covering completely. Lightly press breadcrumbs into fish
- Bake until topping is crisp and golden brown, 18-20 minutes

Serves 4

Grilled Grouper with Lemon Beurre Blanc

When we go to Florida, one of my favorite dishes to make is fresh caught Florida grouper. Even though it's vacation, I like to cook one big, elaborate meal. There's a local seafood store where all the fish is caught that morning and the selection changes according to what was caught that day. I always cross my fingers in hopes that there will be grouper. This meaty white fish is delicious and can hold up on the grill or roasted in the oven. The simple sauce is so good you'll want to lick the plate when you're done.

Grouper:
2-2 1/2 lb grouper fillet, whole or cut
into 4 or 6 smaller fillets, skin removed
1 T olive oil
salt and pepper

Sauce:
4 medium shallots, minced
1/3 cup white wine
1/4 cup seasoned rice vinegar
juice from 1 lemon
1/2 cup (1 stick) unsalted butter cut into 8 pieces

- Preheat grill to medium/high heat
- Brush oil on both sides of fish. Season with salt and pepper. Grill skin side down, 7 minutes. Flip and repeat
- Remove from heat, place on a serving platter and cover with foil to keep warm
- In a skillet over medium/high heat, cook shallots in wine and vinegar. Bring to a boil and cook until reduced by half. Add lemon juice. Pour off liquid so that only shallots remain in the pan. Add butter 1 piece at a time, whisking constantly. Sauce will become thick and emulsified. Season with salt and pepper to taste
- Pour over fish

Serves 4-6

Roasted Sea Bass with Pesto Rub

Jim and I were at a dinner party last year and had the most interesting dish. Estelle, the hostess, is from France and Alberto, the host, is from Spain. Estelle said she Makesthis all the time. It's a traditional Spanish dish, but she doesn't follow a formal recipe. She just uses her culinary instincts, a sign of a good cook. Well, I tried to use my culinary instincts in re-creating the dish and every Sunday night last summer I made it this way and that. My final recipe, the Amy version, is a little different because I added fresh basil.

1/2 cup (packed) basil
1/2 cup (packed) flat leaf parsley
juice of 1 lemon
1 garlic clove, minced
1 T olive oil
2 lb Chilean sea bass fillet

- Preheat oven to 400°
- In a food processor, combine basil, parsley, lemon juice and garlic. Pulse to combine; slowly add olive oil and puree. Season with salt and pepper to taste
- Place sea bass skin side down in a lightly oiled, 8" square baking dish. Place pesto rub evenly over fish
- Roast 15-18 minutes. Fish will be very fragrant when done

Serves 4-6

Flounder with Two Cheese Crumb-Crust

I created this weeknight dinner recipe because I loved the salmon with mustard-crumb crust so much. I always have these ingredients in my pantry, and it's so simple and healthy to make. When the two cheeses cook with the bread crumbs, they get a rich and crunchy flavor.
I like to serve it with a green salad or a sautéed green vegetable such as spinach or broccoli rabe.

2 lbs flounder fillets (4-8 fillets)
1/2 cup Parmesan cheese, freshly grated
1/4 cup Gruyere cheese, freshly grated
1/2 cup bread crumbs (fresh)
2 T unsalted butter, melted
1 T olive oil
1 T flat leaf parsley, chopped
1 garlic clove, minced

- Preheat oven to 425°
- Season fish with salt and pepper and place in a 13x9" baking dish. Set aside
- In a food processor combine Parmesan, Gruyere, bread crumbs, melted butter, olive oil, parsley and garlic to make a heavy crumb mixture. Distribute evenly over fillets (fillets will overlap a little). Bake for 15 minutes until fish is cooked and topping is golden
- Let rest for 5 minutes, then serve

Serves 4

Fillet of Sole with Almonds, Capers, and Lemon

This is another weeknight dinner in our house. It's quick and easy and I always have the ingredients on hand. Sole is a delicate white fish, so be gentle when you cook it and do not overcook! It will lose all its flavor and texture.

1 cup flour
salt and pepper
8 grey sole fillets (1 1/2-2 lbs)
3 1/2 T unsalted butter
2 T canola oil
1/4 cup sliced almonds
1/4 cup capers
1 small lemon, sliced paper thin

- Place flour, salt and pepper in a shallow bowl. Dredge fish in flour mixture and transfer to a plate
- In a large skillet, over high heat combine 1 tablespoon butter and 1 tablespoon oil. Cook four fillets at a time for 3-4 minutes, turning once. Repeat with remaining oil, butter and fish and transfer to a serving platter
- Reduce heat to medium; add remaining butter, almonds, capers and lemon. Cook until almonds are toasted, 2-3. Pour over fish

Serves 4-6

Scallops with Lemon-Mustard Sauce

I love the clean flavor of sea scallops, and this recipe is another weeknight staple in our house. Again, sticking with the lemon-mustard theme, I always have the ingredients. Cooking the scallops from beginning to end takes all of 15 minutes. You can serve this over rice for a more substantial meal.

1 lb sea scallops, patted dry
1/2 cup flour
1/2 t salt
1/2 t pepper
1 T olive oil
2 T unsalted butter
juice of 1 lemon
2 T water
1 t Dijon mustard

- In a medium bowl, combine flour with salt and pepper. Dredge scallops in flour mixture shaking off excess
- In a large skillet over medium/high heat sauté scallops in oil until brown and just cooked through, 3 minutes per side. Remove scallops and transfer to a serving platter
- In same skillet over medium/low heat whisk butter, lemon juice, 2 tablespoons water and mustard and scrape up any brown bits. Simmer until sauce thickens, 2 minutes. Season with salt and pepper to taste
- Spoon over scallops

Serves 4

Soft Shelled Crabs with Tartar Sauce

Growing up, I spent my summers at the beach in southern New Jersey. There was a special restaurant in Atlantic City that my parents always took us to, to celebrate the beginning of the summer. We were definitely the only kids in the place, and all those family dinners at home where we had to have perfect table manners paid off here. Every summer year after year, my brothers and I got the same exact meal. For JB and Tom it was chopped steak (a hamburger with no bun) and Swiss pear dessert, which was a canned pear immersed in whipped cream with chocolate sauce on top. They loved it, I thought "Yuck!" I, on the other hand ordered hearts of lettuce with Gorgonzola, sautéed soft shell crabs, and deep dish blueberry pie. It was a magical meal and one of my first introductions into the world of fine dining.

4 soft shell crabs, cleaned
1/2 cup flour
1/2 t cayenne pepper
1/2 t salt
1/4 t freshly ground pepper
2 T unsalted butter
1 T olive oil

Tartar Sauce
1 cup mayonnaise
1/2 dill pickle, minced
1 shallot, minced
1 T capers
1 T fresh lemon juice

- In a small bowl, mix flour, cayenne, salt and pepper. Dredge each crab in flour mixture, shaking off excess
- In a large skillet over medium/high heat, melt half the butter and half the oil. Add 2 crabs to the pan, top sides down. Cook 3 minutes. With a potato masher, press down lightly on each crab including claws to cook evenly. Turn crabs over and cook an additional 3 minutes. Repeat with remaining butter, oil and crabs
- Tartar Sauce: In a small bowl, combine all ingredients. Serve with crabs

Serves 4

Shrimp Burgers

Who doesn't like a burger? But, it doesn't always have to be made out of meat. I actually think these shrimp burgers are more like crab cakes with shrimp. No need for a bun, just some tartar sauce, a good squeeze of lemon and a green salad.

1 lb cooked shrimp, chopped
3 scallions, trimmed and chopped
1 large celery stalk, chopped
2 T flat leaf parsley, chopped
1 1/2 t lemon zest
3 T mayonnaise

1 cup bread crumbs (fresh)
1 large egg, lightly beaten
1/2 t seafood seasoning
dash hot sauce
2 T canola oil

- In a large bowl, combine shrimp, scallions, celery, parsley, lemon zest, mayonnaise, bread crumbs, egg, seafood seasoning and hot sauce. Season with salt and pepper. Place half the mixture in a food processor and pulse until finely chopped. Combine with remaining mixture. Divide into four patties
- In a large skillet, heat 1 tablespoon oil over medium/high heat. Cook burgers two at a time, until nicely browned, 2 minutes per side. Repeat with the remaining oil and burgers. Drain on paper towels.
- Serve with lettuce, tomato and tartar sauce (page 158)

Serves 4

Grilled Scallop, Corn and Bacon Burgers

This is a very interesting recipe because there are few ingredients, but it packs a wallop of flavor. It's a great summertime dish and if the corn is just picked, it Makesthe burger unbelievably sweet and fresh while the bacon and the grilling add a smoky flavor.

3 ears of corn
1 1/2 lbs sea scallops, coarsely chopped
6 slices of bacon cooked, drained and crumbled
1 T fresh sage, chopped
1 1/2 t salt
1/2 T fresh ground pepper

- Wrap each ear of corn in a wet paper towel and microwave on high 4 minutes. Cut kernels from the cob to make 1 1/2cups
- In a food processor, process 1/2 of corn kernels and 1/3 of the scallops to a paste. Place corn /scallop mixture in a medium bowl and combine with corn kernels, chopped scallops, bacon, sage, salt and pepper. Divide into six patties. Cover and refrigerate 30 minutes
- Heat grill to medium/high. Brush oil on each patty and grill 3-4 minutes per side until charred and cook through
- Serve with lettuce, tomato and tartar sauce (page 158)

Serves 6

<u>Brunch</u>

Sour Cream Coffee Cake

When I started dating my husband, Jim, I was invited to his parent's house for our first Christmas together. It was a magical holiday for me, being included in his family's traditions that I would eventually adapt as my own. On Christmas morning, while we opened gifts around the tree, his mom served warm sour cream coffee cake and hot chocolate. Not only is this coffee cake delicious, but it's now a great tradition for us and perhaps your family too!

Topping:
1/2 cup (1 stick) unsalted
butter, cut up
1/3 cup packed light brown sugar
3 T sugar
1 cup flour
1/4 t cinnamon
Cake:
1/2 cup (1 stick) unsalted butter
1 cup sugar

2 large eggs
2 t vanilla
1 cup sour cream
2 cups flour
1 t baking powder
1/4 t baking soda
1 t salt

- Preheat oven to 350°
- Topping: In a medium bowl with two knives or clean fingers, combine all ingredients until it resembles coarse crumbs. Set aside
- Cake: In a large bowl with an electric mixer beat butter and sugar until light and fluffy. Beat in eggs, vanilla and sour cream until combined. Sift together flour, baking powder, baking soda, and salt and slowly add to batter just to combine
- Spread half of the batter in a buttered and floured bundt pan. Sprinkle half of topping. Add remaining batter and topping
- Bake 35-40 minutes until tester comes out clean

Serves 10-12

Cherry Coffee Cake

My dad's been eating coffee cake for breakfast as long as I can remember. He seems perfectly happy with any dry store bought variety, and he always washes it down with a cup of tea. It gives me great joy to bake him something homemade. He gets so excited and always does the same thing: he cuts the cake in half, saving it for later (or his own private stash). The other half goes in the cake dish for all to share, but everyone knows to leave it for Dad.

Topping:
1/4 cup flour
1/3 cup packed light brown sugar
1/4 cup old fashioned oats
1 t cinnamon
1 T unsalted butter
Cake:
1/2 cup sugar
1 1/2 T unsalted butter
1 cup plain low-fat yogurt
1 1/2 t vanilla

3/4 t almond extract
1 large egg
1 1/2 cups flour
1 t baking powder
1/2 t baking soda
1/4 t salt
1 1/2 cups cherries, pitted

- Preheat oven to 350°
- Topping: In a medium bowl with two knives or clean fingers, combine all ingredients until it resembles coarse meal. Set aside
- Cake: In a large bowl, with an electric mixer, beat sugar and butter until light and fluffy. Beat in yogurt, extracts, and egg until combined. Sift together flour, baking powder, baking soda and salt and slowly add to batter until just combined
- Spread half the batter in bottom of a buttered and floured 8" square baking pan. Place the cherries on top of the batter with half the topping. Add remaining batter and topping
- Bake for 40-45 minutes until tester comes out clean

Serves 8-10

Sticky Buns

I have a confession to make. I love sticky buns, but only the top. When I was little and there were sticky buns in the cake dish, I would sneak into the kitchen long after dinner and eat the top off the sticky buns. Feeling clever, I would pour honey on top thinking no one would notice. The next morning, when my dad was having his cake for breakfast, he would, well, you can imagine his unpleasant surprise. Since I was the good girl, I would tell him my brothers did it and he believed me. I guess I am fessing up 30 years later. Sorry JB and Tom. This cake is for you.

Dough:
1 envelope yeast
1/4 cup sugar
1/2 cup + 2 T warm milk (105° -115°)
1 large egg
3/4 t salt
3 cups flour
5 T unsalted butter, softened
+ more for greasing bowl
Topping:
3/4 cup packed dark brown sugar

1/2 cup light corn syrup
1/2 cup (1 stick) unsalted butter, softened
4 T honey
2/3 cup raisins
Filling:
2 T unsalted butter, melted
1/4 cup sugar
2 t cinnamon

- <u>Dough</u>: In a large bowl dissolve yeast and 1 teaspoon sugar in the warm milk. Let stand until foamy, 10 minutes
- With a wooden spoon, beat in eggs, remaining sugar, salt, flour and butter. Mix until dough begins to pull away from sides of the bowl. Turn out onto lightly floured surface and knead 2-3 minutes until smooth and elastic
- Shape into a ball and transfer to a buttered bowl. Turn to coat, cover and let rise in a warm place, 1 1/2-2 hours, until doubled in size
- <u>Topping</u>: In a small saucepan over medium heat, combine brown sugar, corn syrup and butter stirring constantly until smooth
- Remove from heat. Stir in honey and raisins. Pour into bottom of a buttered 13x9" baking dish

- <u>Filling</u>: Meanwhile, punch down dough and roll out on a floured surface to a 20 x 12" rectangle. Brush with melted butter. Combine sugar and cinnamon. Sprinkle evenly over dough
- Roll up from long side like a jelly roll and cut into 20, 1" slices. Arrange spiral side up over topping, 5 rows with 4 in each row. Cover and let rise in a warm place 1 1/2-2 hours until doubled in size
- Pre-heat oven to 350°. Uncover and bake 30 minutes until buns are golden. Cool in pan 1 minute then invert on serving platter and cool

Serves 20

Banana Bread

Sometimes the best recipes are the simplest ones. I like to keep a bowl of fruit on my kitchen table. When my kids are hungry for a snack, I point to the bowl. When the bananas have seen better days, I make banana bread. The kids love it and the bananas get a second life. Sometimes I put 1/2 cup of mini chocolate chips in the batter. It's not a lot of chocolate, but it goes a long way.

3 ripe bananas
1 cup sugar
1 large egg
4 T (1/2 stick) unsalted butter, melted
1 t vanilla
1 1/2 cups flour

1 t baking soda
1/2 t salt

- Preheat oven to 325°
- In a large bowl with an electric mixer, beat bananas, sugar, egg, butter and vanilla until thoroughly combined. Sift flour, baking soda and salt and slowly add to batter until just combined
- Pour batter into a buttered 9" loaf pan. Bake for 1 hour until tester comes out clean
- Let bread cool in pan for 10 minutes, then turn out onto wire rack

Makes 1 loaf

Chunky Apple Bread

Everyone who tries this bread loves it. It's very simple and straight forward, but delicious especially in the fall when apples are abundant. When you're cutting up the apples, don't make them too big or the bread will not hold together. I know, I've made that mistake too many times.

2 apples, peeled, cored and diced
1 cup sugar
1 1/2 cups flour
1 t baking soda
pinch salt
1/4 t nutmeg

1/4 t cinnamon
1/2 cup (1 stick) unsalted butter, melted
1 large egg, lightly beaten
1 t vanilla

- Preheat oven to 325°
- In a large bowl, combine apples and sugar. Set aside. Mix flour with baking soda, salt, nutmeg, cinnamon and butter. Add to the apple mixture. Combine eggs and vanilla and then add to batter. Pour into a buttered 9" loaf pan
- Bake 1 hour until tester comes out clean
- Cool in pan for 10 minutes, then turn out onto wire rack

Makes 1 loaf

Apple Pancake

Once, when I was at my children's school waiting to pick them up, my friend Courtney asked me if I had any good brunch recipes. She was having a family party for her son and could not find any easy yet impressive dishes. I thought about it for a long time, months, in fact. I became a little obsessed with brunch recipes and I came up with quite a few. So, every casserole in this chapter is dedicated to you, Courtney. You will never have to worry about a brunch menu again!

1 cup whole milk
4 large eggs
3 T sugar
1 t vanilla
1/2 t salt
1/4 t cinnamon
2/3 cup flour

4 T (1/2 stick) unsalted butter
2 apples, peeled, cored, and thinly sliced
3 T packed light brown sugar

- Preheat oven to 425°
- In a large bowl, whisk milk, eggs, sugar, vanilla, salt, cinnamon and flour. Set aside
- Place butter in a 13x 9" baking dish and place in the oven until the butter melts. Add apples to the baking dish spreading out on top of the melted butter. Bake 10 minutes until butter is bubbling on edges and apples begin to soften
- Pour batter over apples and sprinkle brown sugar on top
- Bake 15 minutes until pancake is puffed and golden

Serves 8-10

Thin Swedish Pancakes (Blini's)

My neighbor, Annette, has a Christmas party every year with a Swedish theme. She spent some time in Sweden and has a rich knowledge of the traditions. The food is always as delicious as it is authentic, and my favorite dish of all is the Swedish pancakes. When I asked Annette for the recipe, I admitted I wanted to serve them as the Russian version, called blini's. Annette laughed at my international ambiguity and said either way her kids love them with a little jelly. My kids couldn't agree more.

3 large eggs
2 1/2 cups whole milk
1 cup flour
1/2 t salt
3 T unsalted butter, melted

- In a large bowl, whisk eggs, milk, flour, salt and butter
- Spray a large skillet with non-stick spray and heat over medium heat. Pour approximately 2 tablespoons batter to make a 2-3" diameter pancake. When bubbly and a little dry, flip over. Cook 1 more minute
- Serve with jelly for Swedish version and smoked salmon or caviar and crème fraiche for blini version

Makes approximately 30 pancakes

Catie's French Toast

My mother—in-law, Dottie, knows our kids pretty well. If you ask her to describe our daughter, Catie, one of the first things she'll say is that Catie loves breakfast. Last summer, Dottie and my father-in-law, Jim, were at a charming bed and breakfast in northern Michigan. They had "crème brule french toast" for breakfast and declared it a winner. The owner graciously gave the recipe to Dottie who promptly re-named it "Catie's french toast". Now, Catie looks forward to having "her" french toast whenever she visits grammy and grandpa.

1/2 cup (1 stick) unsalted butter
1 cup packed light brown sugar
2 T corn syrup
1 loaf challah or brioche bread
5 large eggs
1 1/2 cups half and half

1 t vanilla
1 t fresh orange juice
1/4 t salt

- In a small saucepan over medium heat, combine butter, brown sugar and corn syrup until mixture is smooth, stirring constantly. Pour into a 13x9" baking dish
- Cut bread into 1" slices. Trim crust from each slice and arrange over syrup cutting some of the bread into pieces so entire dish is covered. Whisk together eggs, half and half, vanilla, orange juice and salt. Pour over bread
- Cover and refrigerate overnight
- Pre-heat oven to 350°. Uncover and bring to room temperature, 30 minutes. Bake 40 minutes until puffed and edges are golden brown. Sprinkle with confectioners sugar

Serves 8-10

Ham and Cheese Scones

Around the time Jimmy learned to ride a bike, he decided to give ice hockey a try. I thought his practices would be a great time for Jim and Jimmy to have a little one-on-one father-son time. Jim was thrilled until he found out his practice time: Saturday morning at 6:00. Well, big Jim was a good sport and little Jimmy learned how to ice skate really well. I wanted to send my boys off with a good, nutritious breakfast, but I didn't want to get up in pitch-black darkness to make it. Thus, the ham and cheese scone was born. I'd make a batch and freeze it. Take two out of the freezer the night before and the next morning they're good to go!

2 cups flour + more for dusting
1 T baking powder
1 t salt
1/2 t paprika
3/4 cup (1 1/2 sticks) unsalted butter
3 large eggs
1/2 cup heavy cream

1 cup (4 oz) Cheddar cheese, grated
7 oz lean ham steak, cubed

- Preheat oven to 400°
- In a food processor, combine flour, baking powder, salt and paprika. Add butter and pulse until it resembles coarse crumbs. Add eggs, cream and cheese and pulse until just combined. Turn out onto a floured surface and knead in ham
- On a parchment lined baking sheet, form dough into a 9" circle, With a knife dipped in flour, cut into 8 wedges, keeping the circle intact
- Bake 25-30 minutes until crusty and golden. Remove from oven, cut immediately along wedge lines again to make individual scones

Serves 8

Sausage, Egg and Cheese Strata

This dish is another Currie family holiday tradition. After the presents were opened on Christmas morning, we'd have breakfast consisting of a green grape and strawberry fruit salad (red & green, get it?) and sausage, egg and cheese strata. Except, they called this delicious casserole "egg thing". The best thing about "egg thing' is that you make it the day before and pop it in the oven just before serving. I've made this dish many, many times since that first Christmas, and I recently began to substitute lean ham instead of sausage. It's a little healthier and very tasty. Either way it's great, just don't call it "egg thing".

1 lb bulk breakfast sausage
6 slices white bread, crusts removed, cubed
1 cup (4 oz) sharp Cheddar cheese, grated

2 cups whole milk
6 large eggs
1 t mustard
1 t salt

- In a large skillet over medium/high heat, cook and drain sausage. In a 13x9" baking dish, layer bread cubes, sausage, and then cheese. Whisk milk, eggs, mustard and salt and pour over bread, sausage and cheese
- Cover and refrigerate overnight
- Preheat oven to 350º
- Bring strata to room temperature, 30 minutes. Bake 40-45 minutes until puffy and golden

Serves 8-10

Spinach and Gruyere Strata

I liked the sausage, egg, and cheese strata so much I came up with several variations. This spinach and Gruyere strata is very tasty and perfect for vegetarians. It also adds a bit of color to a potentially bland looking spread (brunch dishes tends to all look the same color: beige) this dish is also terrific for a ladies lunch. Add a salad and you're set.

1 medium onion, chopped
2 T unsalted butter
1 t salt
1/2 t pepper
1/4 t nutmeg
10 oz package frozen chopped spinach, thawed and squeezed dry
1 French baguette, cubed
1 1/2 cups (6 oz) Gruyere cheese, grated

1/2 cup (2 oz) Parmesan cheese, freshly grated
2 cups whole milk
6 large eggs
1 T Dijon mustard

- In a large skillet over medium heat, sauté onion in butter until soft, 5 minutes. Add salt, pepper and nutmeg. Stir in spinach and remove from heat
- Arrange bread, spinach and both cheeses in a 13x9" baking dish. Whisk milk, eggs and mustard and pour over bread, spinach and cheese
- Cover and refrigerate overnight
- Preheat oven to 350°. Bring strata to room temperature, 30 minutes
- Bake 40-45 minutes until puffy and golden

Serves 8-10

Smoked Salmon and Dill Strata

Several years ago, Jim's parents, took a trip to Alaska. I knew they had a great time when we received a large cooler in the mail filled with freshly caught (by them!) Alaskan salmon. It was about 25 lbs worth, all beautifully cleaned and filleted. I went into salmon overdrive, cooking old favorites and trying new ones. One of my new endeavors was gravlax, which is a Swedish delicacy similar in texture and flavor to smoked salmon. I wasn't thrilled with the results, so when I saw that this was the topic on my favorite live TV cooking show, I decided to call in and explain my dilemma. Coincidentally, Dottie was watching the same show and she heard me recount *her* trip to Alaska, *her* fishing expedition and my dismal gravlax. So, my 15 minutes of fame was hers too. I don't think I'll be making gravlax any more, but smoked salmon is a nice alternative, especially in this strata.

1 large potato, peeled and diced
2 T unsalted butter
2 shallots, minced
1 French baguette, cubed
4 oz smoked salmon, chopped
3 T fresh chives, minced
3 T fresh dill, minced

6 large eggs
1 1/2 cups half and half
1/2 cup sour cream
1 1/2 t Dijon mustard
salt and pepper

- In a large skillet over medium/high heat, sauté potatoes in butter, 10 minutes. Add shallots and cook another 2 minutes. Remove from heat. Place potato mixture in a 13x9" baking dish
- In a large bowl, mix bread, salmon, chives and dill. Layer on top of potatoes. Whisk eggs, half and half, sour cream, mustard, salt and pepper and pour over mixture
- Cover and refrigerate overnight
- Preheat oven to 350º. Bring strata to room temperature, 30 minutes
- Bake 40-45 minutes until puffy and golden

Serves 8-10

Red Onion Quiche

This is another Currie family tradition rich in history. When Jim was growing up, his entire street would go caroling at Christmastime. Afterwards, the block would convene at a neighbor's house for a light supper. Jim's mom always brought red onion quiche. I like to make homemade piecrust but frozen or refrigerated is fine too. You can also substitute the onions for anything that strikes your fancy: spinach, bacon (cooked), mushrooms (sautéed). Be creative or stick with tradition!

9" pie crust (page 16)
2 large eggs, beaten
1/4 cup (1 oz) Gruyere cheese, freshly grated
1/4 cup (1oz) Parmesan cheese, freshly grated
1 T flour
1/2 large red onion, thinly sliced
1 cup half and half
pinch of nutmeg
1/2 t salt
dash of pepper

- Preheat oven to 425°
- Place pie crust into a 9" pie or tart pan. Brush with a bit of the beaten egg and place in freezer for 30 minutes
- Preheat oven to 425°
- Mix cheeses with flour, spread in pie shell. Cover with onions. Whisk half and half, remaining eggs, nutmeg, salt and pepper and pour over onions
- Bake 35-40 minutes until golden brown

Serves 6-8

Kielbasa in Apricot-Mustard Glaze

I was at a baby shower several years ago and I had kielbasa sausage cooked in apricot jam. It was so delicious; smoky and sweet at the same time. I really wanted the recipe, but didn't know the hostess well enough to ask. I got home and went to work. I came up with this recipe, which I like even more because the herbs add an even greater depth of flavor. One cautionary word, though; if you're planning to serve this to children as well as adults, just stick with the apricot preserves so it's not too spicy or seasoned.

1 lb Kielbasa, cut into 1/2" slices
1/2 cup apricot preserves
1/4 cup sweet-hot mustard
1 T fresh rosemary, chopped
1 t fresh thyme, chopped

- Preheat oven 400°
- In a medium bowl, combine preserves, mustard, rosemary and thyme. Toss Kielbasa in mixture to coat evenly
- Place in a single layer on a baking sheet lined with non-stick aluminum foil. Bake 20 minutes, turning after 10 until brown and bubbly
- Serve immediately

Serves 6-8

Cheesy Sausage Roll

If you really want to impress your guests while keeping your sanity, this will do the trick. It can be made in advance and frozen, it can sit on a buffet for hours at room temperature, and it goes with almost anything.

12 oz bulk breakfast sausage
1 small onion, chopped
1 celery stalk, chopped
1 garlic clove, minced
3 oz cream cheese
1 cup (4oz) Cheddar cheese, grated
2 scallions, trimmed and chopped

2 T flat leaf parsley, chopped
1 tube (8 oz) refrigerated
crescent rolls
1 large egg, lightly beaten

- Preheat oven to 350°
- In a large skillet over medium heat cook sausage until brown, 10 minutes. Drain on paper towels reserving 1 tablespoon of drippings in pan. In same skillet over medium heat, sauté onion and celery until soft, 5 minutes. Add sausage and cook another minute to combine. Add cheeses, scallions and parsley. Reduce heat to low and stir until cheese is melted. Set aside
- Unroll crescent dough on a baking sheet lined with non-stick aluminum foil. Press perforations together and roll into a 12x10" rectangle. Spoon sausage mixture evenly over rectangle leaving a 1" boarder all around edge. Roll lengthwise to form a jelly roll. Bring the two ends together to make a ring.
- Brush dough with egg and bake 20-25 minutes until golden brown

Serves 8-10

Desserts - Cookies and Bars

Chocolate Chunk Cookies

This is my neighbor, Karen's recipe. She claims to be the world's worst cook. Why include her chocolate chunk cookie recipe? Quit simply, it's terrific. This was Karen's favorite recipe from her childhood. She knew it by heart when I asked her for it. It's not much different than the famous Toll House cookies but slightly crispier. It's partly because these cookies are cooked at a higher heat for a shorter period of time. By the way, Karen, you really are a good cook. Just ask my son, William!

3/4 cup (1 1/2 sticks) unsalted butter, softened
1/2 cup sugar
1 cup packed light brown sugar
2 large eggs
1 t vanilla

2 cups flour
1 t salt
1 t baking soda
12 oz bag semisweet chocolate chunks

- Preheat oven to 375°
- In a large bowl with an electric mixer, beat butter and both sugars until light and fluffy. Beat in eggs and vanilla until combined. Sift together flour, salt and baking soda and slowly add to batter until just combined. Fold in chocolate chunks
- Place golf-ball size mounds of dough 3" apart on parchment lined baking sheets
- Bake 10-12 minutes until golden brown
- Cool on wire racks

Makes approximately 2 dozen

Milk Chocolate Chip Sugar Cookies

My husband, Jim, declares that this is a very satisfying cookie. It's actually a hybrid of sorts between a vanilla sugar cookie and a chocolate chip cookie. It seems like such a logical combination, but I'd never seen it before. It's now a staple in my repertory.

1 cup (2 sticks) unsalted butter, softened
2/3 cup sugar
1/2 cup packed light brown sugar
1 large egg
2 t vanilla
2 1/2 cups flour

1/2 t baking soda
1/4 t cinnamon
1/4 t salt
12 oz bag milk
chocolate chips

- Preheat oven to 350°
- In a large bowl with an electric mixer, beat butter and both sugars until light and fluffy. Beat in egg and vanilla until combined. Sift together flour, baking soda, cinnamon and salt and slowly add to batter until just combined. Fold in chocolate chips
- Place golf-ball size mounds of dough 3" apart on parchment lined baking sheets
- Bake 10-12 minutes until golden brown
- Cool on wire racks

Makes approximately 2 dozen

"Famous Department Store" Cookies

One day my Mom called me all excited. She got the recipe for the "famous department store" cookies with an interesting story to go with it. The story goes like this: A mother and her daughter were having lunch at a well known department store. They ordered the cookies for dessert and liked them so much, they asked for the recipe. The waitress said the recipe would cost $2.00 and she could add it onto her store credit card. Several weeks later when the bill arrived, she was charged $200. When she questioned the bill, the store blamed her for the miscommunication. She was so disgruntled she re-told her story along with the recipe and e-mailed it to everyone she knew and instructed them to e-mail it to their friends and so on. Well, it found its way to my mom and she sent it to me. We both decided that it's probably one of those urban myths, but the cookie is out of this world.

2 1/2 cups old fashioned oats
4 oz milk chocolate bar
1 cup (2 sticks) unsalted butter, softened
1 cup sugar
1 cup packed light brown sugar
2 large eggs
1 t vanilla

2 cups flour
1/2 t salt
1 t baking powder
12 oz bag semisweet chocolate chips
1 1/2 cups walnuts, toasted

- Preheat oven to 350°
- Place oatmeal in a food processor and process into a powder. Set aside. Place Hershey bar in the food processor and process into a powder. Set aside
- In a large bowl with an electric mixer, beat butter and both sugars until light and fluffy. Beat in egg and vanilla until combined. Sift together flour, salt and baking powder and slowly add to batter until just combined. Fold in oatmeal, Hershey bar, chocolate chips and nuts
- Place golf-ball size mounds of dough 3" apart on parchment lined baking sheets

- Bake 10-12 minutes until golden brown
- Cool on wire racks

Makes approximately 2 dozen

Cookies from Heaven

One day, my dear friend Maria was driving around doing errands. She was listening to the radio when she heard a recipe for eggless chocolate chip cookies. They sounded so interesting, she hastily wrote the recipe on the back of her shopping list while driving. Sometime after that, I was at a luncheon at her house and she had these unbelievable cookies. She told me the story apologizing the whole time because she wasn't sure if she got the recipe right. Well, I know she got the recipe right. They are simply heavenly.

3/4 cup (1 1/2 sticks) unsalted butter, softened
1/2 cup sugar
1/3 cup packed light brown sugar
1 t vanilla
2 T whole milk
3 T corn syrup

1 1/2 cup flour
1/4 t salt
3/4 t baking soda
1 cup pecans or walnut, toasted
1 cup semisweet chocolate chips

- Preheat oven to 350°
- In a large bowl with an electric mixer, beat butter and both sugars until light and fluffy. Beat in vanilla, milk and corn syrup to combine. Sift together flour, salt and baking soda and slowly add to batter until just combined. Fold in nuts and chocolate chips. Cover and chill 30 minutes
- Drop 1 tablespoon of dough 3" apart on parchment lined baking sheets
- Bake 8-10 minutes until thin, crispy and golden brown
- Cool on wire racks

Makes approximately 3 1/2 dozen

Chocolate Mint Cookies

For those of you who like the combination of chocolate and mint, this is for you. They taste very similar to a certain cookie sold by a young girls' organization. But you don't have to wait for your door bell to ring to have them, now you can make them whenever you want.

3/4 cup (1 1/2 sticks) unsalted butter, softened
1 cup sugar
1 large egg
1/2 t vanilla
3/4 t peppermint extract
1 1/2 cups flour
3/4 cup cocoa powder
1/4 t salt
6 oz semisweet chocolate

- In a large bowl with an electric mixer, beat butter and sugar until light and fluffy. Beat in egg, vanilla and peppermint extract until combined. Sift together flour, cocoa and salt and slowly add to batter until just combined
- Divide dough in half. Form two logs, 2" in diameter. Wrap in plastic and chill 2 hours
- Preheat oven to 350°
- Unwrap logs and roll on countertop to smooth out. Cut crosswise into 1/4" rounds and place 2" apart on parchment lined baking sheets
- Bake 12-15 minutes
- Cool on wire racks
- Melt chocolate in a double boiler. Dip a fork in the chocolate and drizzle over cookies in a zigzag pattern. Refrigerate cookies until chocolate is set

Makes approximately 3 1/2 dozen

Turtles

I was invited to a cookie exchange several years ago and I was a little intimidated because I knew the women participating in the exchange were all really good cooks. I was planning on making a simple chewy chocolate cookie when I noticed that I had a bag of caramels left over from caramel apples at Halloween. I added the caramels and a few nuts, and this new cookie instantly reminded me of those deliciously chocolaty, caramel turtle candies. I felt pretty good going to the cookie exchange and when I brought home my plate of assorted cookies, my kids only wanted to know where all the turtles went.

Cookies:
1/2 cup (1 stick) unsalted butter, softened
2/3 cup sugar
1 large egg, divided
2 T whole milk
1 t vanilla
1 cup flour

1/3 cup cocoa powder
1/4 t salt
1/2 cup chopped pecans
Caramel:
10 caramels, unwrapped
2 T heavy cream

- In a large bowl with an electric mixer, beat butter and sugar until light and fluffy. Beat in egg yolk, milk and vanilla to combine. Sift together flour, cocoa and salt and slowly add to batter until just combined. Form dough into a disk, wrap in plastic and chill 30 minutes
- Preheat oven 350°
- Roll tablespoons of dough into balls, coat with egg white and roll in nuts. Place on parchment lined baking sheets baking sheets, 2" apart. Press thumb into center of cookies leaving a depression
- Bake 10-12 minutes
- Remove from oven and press center of cookies again with the handle end of a wooden spoon
- In a small saucepan over low heat, combine caramels and cream until melted, stirring occasionally. Spoon caramel mixture into centers of cookies and cool completely

Makes approximately 2 1/2 dozen

Cocoa Hermits

This little gem from my stepmother's family is a year round favorite. Barbara's great grandma Lamp used to say "One batch of cocoa hermits feeds 50 hungry hounds". This cookie is also a favorite among the littlest up and coming bakers because even the smallest fingers can make a hermit with no experience necessary.

1 cup (2 sticks) unsalted butter, softened
1 1/3 cups sugar
4 large eggs
1/2 cup cocoa powder
4 cups flour

2 t baking powder
1 t salt
2 t cinnamon
15 oz box raisins
25 maraschino cherries, halved

- Pre-heat oven to 350°
- In a large bowl, with an electric mixer, beat butter and sugar until light and fluffy. Beat in eggs until well combined. Sift together cocoa, flour, baking powder, salt and cinnamon and slowly add to batter until just combined. Fold in raisins
- Drop 1 tablespoon of dough 2" apart on parchment lined baking sheets. Place half of a cherry on top of each cookie
- Bake 10-12 minutes until set and dry
- Cool on wire racks

Makes approximately 4 dozen or 50 cookies

Peanut Butter Cookies

I have to admit, these are not my favorite cookies. I just don't really like peanut butter. Our daughter, Catie, could put peanut butter on anything and enjoy it. I get so weary of making peanut butter sandwiches day in and day out. But every once in a while I get a craving for a peanut butter cookie. Then I'm glad I have my warehouse size jar of peanut butter in the pantry. A note to peanut butter cookie fans, a lot of recipes call for chunky peanut butter. I think smooth is so much better with the addition of dry roasted chopped peanuts. This brings out a better depth of flavor in the cookie.

1/2 cup (1 stick) unsalted butter, softened
1 cup packed light brown sugar
1 large egg
1 t vanilla
1 cup smooth peanut butter
1 1/2 cups flour
1/2 t baking soda
1/2 t salt
1/2 cup dry roasted, unsalted peanuts, chopped

- Preheat oven to 350°
- In a large bowl with an electric mixer, beat butter and sugar until light and fluffy. Beat in egg, vanilla and peanut butter until well combined. Sift together flour, baking soda and salt and slowly add to batter until just combined. Fold in chopped peanuts. Cover and chill 30 minutes
- Place golf-ball size mounds of dough, 3" apart on parchment lined baking sheets. Flatten with a fork in a crisscross pattern
- Bake 12-15 minutes until golden brown
- Cool on wire racks

Makes approximately 2 1/2 dozen

Flourless Peanut Butter and Chocolate Chip Cookies

When my husband Jim was little — around 10 — he and his buddy, Tony snuck down to the main drag in their town and went to the candy store. They each had $1.00, which was a lot back then. They spent every last penny on candy and they ate every last bite before they got home. Well, he must have downed quite a few peanut butter cups because every time I make this recipe, he recounts this story with a wince. He's the only one I know that doesn't like these cookies.

1 cup smooth peanut butter
1 cup packed light brown sugar
1 large egg
1 t baking soda
1 t vanilla
1 cup milk chocolate chips

- Preheat oven to 350°
- In a large bowl, with an electric mixer, combine peanut butter, brown sugar, egg, baking soda and vanilla. Fold in chocolate chips
- Drop 1 tablespoon of dough 3" apart on parchment lined baking sheets. Flatten slightly with the bottom of a glass
- Bake 10-12 minutes until puffed and golden brown, but still soft
- Cool on wire racks

Makes approximately 3 dozen

Very Best Oatmeal Cookies

I generally do not like to label any of my recipes the "very best". These oatmeal cookies, however are so good, others don't hold a candle to them. A while ago I was complaining to my friend Nancy that I didn't have an oatmeal cookie recipe that I really liked and she gave me this one. It has the perfect combination that I strive for in a cookie: Chewy and crispy. Sometimes I like to substitute the raisins with another dried fruit like cranberries, cherries, or apricots.

1 cup (2 sticks) unsalted butter, softened
2 cups (1 box) light brown sugar
2 large eggs
1 t vanilla
2 cups flour
1 t salt

1 t baking soda
1 t baking powder
2 cups old fashioned oats
1 cup raisins

- In a large bowl with an electric mixer, beat butter and sugar until light and fluffy. Beat in eggs and vanilla until combined. Sift together flour, salt, baking soda and powder and slowly add to batter until just combined. Fold in oatmeal and raisins. Cover and chill 30 minutes
- Preheat oven to 350°
- Place golf-ball size mounds of dough 3" apart on parchment lined baking sheets
- Bake 8-10 minutes until golden brown
- Cool on wire racks

Makes approximately 2 dozen

Chewy Molasses Cookies

I love molasses cookies, but they must be chewy. It's just a personal preference but to me it's not worth the effort if it doesn't have the right consistency. This cookie gets it just right.

1/2 cup applesauce
6 T (3/4 stick) unsalted butter, softened
1 1/4 cups sugar
1/4 cup unsulphured molasses
1 large egg
2 cups flour
2 t baking soda

1 t cinnamon
1/2 t salt
1/2 t ginger
1/2 t cloves

- Spoon applesauce onto several layers of paper towels to absorb liquid. Let rest for 5 minutes then scrape with a spatula into a bowl. Set aside
- In a large bowl with an electric mixer, beat butter and 1 cup sugar until light and fluffy. Beat in molasses, egg and applesauce until combined. Sift together flour, baking soda, cinnamon, salt, ginger and cloves and slowly add to the batter until just combined. Cover and chill for 30 minutes
- Preheat oven to 375°
- With moistened hands shape dough into 1 1/2" balls. Roll in remaining 1/4 cup sugar and drop dough 3" apart on parchment lined baking sheets. Flatten cookies with the bottom of a glass
- Bake 8-10 minutes until puffed
- Cool on wire racks

Makes approximately 3 dozen

Snickerdoodles

This is my daughter, Catie's favorite cookie. She can never remember the name, so she calls them "those cinnamon cookies". I'm always happy to make them for her because I really like them, too. In fact, this is a great recipe to make with kids because the dough is pliable, like clay. They don't have to be perfect circles. Let your kids get their creative juices flowing. They'll still taste great.

4 T (1/2 stick) unsalted butter, softened
1 cup + 3 T sugar
1 T corn syrup
1 large egg
1 t vanilla
1 3/4 cups flour

1/2 t baking soda
1/2 t cream of tartar
2 t cinnamon

- Preheat oven to 375°
- In a large bowl with an electric mixer, beat butter and 1 cup sugar until light and fluffy. Beat in corn syrup, egg and vanilla to combine. Sift together flour, baking soda and cream of tarter and slowly add to batter just to combine
- With moist hands, shape dough into 1 1/2" balls. Combine 3 tablespoon sugar with cinnamon. Roll cookies in mixture
- Drop dough 3" apart on parchment lined baking sheets. Flatten cookies with bottom of a glass
- Bake 8-10 minutes until golden brown
- Cool on wire racks

Makes approximately 2 dozen

Pecan Shortbread

We didn't have a lot of cookies in our house growing up, but my mother loved pecan shortbread cookies, so there was always a box of those to be found. I remember thinking they were a little bland, but out of cookie desperation I grew to love them too. This homemade version is so much better. It's basically shortbread dough with toasted pecans.
Mom really likes my homemade version, but when I go home for a visit, I can still always find a box of pecan shortbread cookies!

3/4 cup pecans, toasted　　　　　*1 1/4 cups flour*
2/3 cup + 2 T confectioners sugar　　*1/2 t salt*
1/2 cup (1 stick) unsalted butter, softened　*1/4 t baking powder*
1/2 t vanilla
1 large egg, separated

- In a food processor, pulse pecans with 2 tablespoons confectioners sugar until finely ground. Set aside
- In a large bowl with an electric mixer beat butter, 2/3 *cup* confectioners sugar and vanilla until light and fluffy. Beat in egg yolk until combined, then pecan mixture. Sift together flour, salt and baking powder and slowly add to batter until just combined (Add 1 tablespoon of ice water if mixture seems too dry)
- Form dough into a disk, wrap in plastic and chill 1 hour
- Preheat oven to 325°
- On a lightly floured surface, roll out dough to a 1/4" thickness. Cut with a 2-3" round cookie cutter and place 2" apart on parchment lined baking sheets
- Beat egg white until frothy and brush tops of cookies
- Bake 15-20 minutes until tops are golden brown
- Cool on wire racks

Makes approximately 2 1/2 dozen

Mexican Wedding Cookies

This is one of my earliest childhood memories; sitting in my Nanny's kitchen and watching her cook. She was like a tornado, cooking and baking so many things at once, I don't know how she was able to keep track. Mexican wedding cookies were in her repertory. My job was to roll them in the powdered sugar right after they came out of the oven. But they were really too hot, and Nanny didn't want me to burn my fingers. So she would stand over me and do it herself making me think that I was doing all the work. The funny thing is, I do that all the time with my kids when we bake together and they are convinced they're doing an excellent job too!

2 cups flour
1/2 cup confectioners sugar + more for rolling
1 cup chopped pecans
1 t vanilla
1/2 cup (1 stick) unsalted butter, softened

- Preheat oven to 350°
- In a food processor, pulse flour, sugar and pecans to a coarse consistency. Add vanilla and butter and pulse until mixture turns into dough (add 1 tablespoon ice water if mixture seems too dry)
- With moist hands, shape dough into 1" balls. Drop dough 2" apart on parchment lined baking sheets
- Bake 10-12 minutes until set and golden brown
- Roll in confectioners sugar while still warm

Makes approximately 3 dozen

Toasted Almond Macaroons

Macaroons have a bad reputation. Everyone thinks they are made out of sweetened shredded coconut. Well, not so! In the Jewish tradition, during the Passover holiday, traditional macaroons are made with almonds and they are delicious. I make these cookies all the time, and they go especially well as an accompaniment to fresh fruit.

4 1/2 cups confectioners sugar
2 cups whole almonds, toasted
1/2 cup flour
1 cup chopped almonds, toasted
6 large egg whites
1/4 t salt
1/2 t almond extract

- Preheat oven to 400°
- In a food processor in two batches, combine sugar and whole almonds until they form a powder. Transfer to a bowl, sift in flour, and then stir in chopped almonds. Set aside
- In a large bowl with an electric mixer, beat egg whites and salt until stiff but not dry. Mix in almond extract, then fold in nut mixture
- Spoon batter by tablespoons onto parchment lined baking sheets
- Bake 10-12 minutes until puffed and golden brown
- Cool on wire racks

Makes approximately 4 dozen

Lemon Butter Cookies

One thing that I've grown to love is having friends over for coffee, tea, brunch, lunch, whatever. In my house any excuse will do to get together. If someone's kids are home, they come. If all the kids are in school, well then it's a party! I'm always challenged to serve something special when they arrive because this is our break from the day. It should be celebrated even if it is a fleeting moment. These cookies are great with a cup of coffee or with a fruit salad for dessert. I try to keep a batch ready to go in the freezer, but they never last too long.

3/4 cup (1 1/2 sticks) unsalted butter, softened
2/3 cup sugar
zest from 2 lemons
1 large egg
1 t vanilla
2 cups flour
confectioners sugar for dusting

- In a large bowl with an electric mixer, beat butter and sugar until light and fluffy. Beat in lemon zest, egg and vanilla until combined. Sift flour and slowly add until just combined. Form the dough into a disc, wrap in plastic and chill 1 hour
- Preheat oven to 375°
- On a lightly floured surface, roll out dough to a 1/4" thickness. Cut with a 2-3" cookie cutter (round, heart shape, star, etc) and place 2" apart on parchment lined baking sheets
- Bake 8-10 minutes until edges are golden brown
- Sift confectioners sugar over cookies while still warm

Makes approximately 3 dozen

Vanilla Thins

This is a very plain cookie, and I mean that in the most complimentary way. Planning a menu is a lot like putting an outfit together. You can't mix a striped top with a plaid bottom. The same idea applies to menu planning. If everything is over the top, it's hard to stay focused and appreciate each dish. These cookies provide a great balance when planning dessert. For example, if you're serving triple chocolate caramel nut marshmallow ice cream sundaes, the perfect accompaniment would be vanilla thins. Of course you can always keep everything simple. They go beautifully with fruit too!

1/4 cup (1/2 stick) unsalted butter, softened
1/4 cup sugar
1 large egg
1/2 t vanilla
1/4 cup flour+ 1 t
1/8 t salt

- Preheat oven to 350°
- In a large bowl with an electric mixer, beat butter and sugar until light and fluffy. Beat in egg and vanilla until combined. Sift together flour and salt and slowly add to batter until just combined. Drop 1 scant tablespoon of dough 3" apart on parchment lined baking sheets
- Bake 6-8 minutes until edges are golden brown
- Cool on baking sheets 2 minutes then transfer wire racks

Makes approximately 2 1/2 dozen

BB's Ice Box Cookies

Picture this: Six adult children home for the holidays on a clandestine mission. Ice box cookie dough is chilling in the refrigerator. A midnight raid ensues. The challenge? To eat as much dough as possible without mom noticing the next day. This story, told to me by my stepmother, Barbara, is as much a family tradition as baking and decorating the cookies themselves. I am also told there is a contest with rewards given for neatness, creativity, and perseverance in the overall cookie making process. This is what I call a baking extravaganza!

Cookies:
1 1/2 cups (3 sticks) unsalted butter, softened
1 cup packed light brown sugar
1 cup sugar
3 large eggs
4 1/2 cups flour
1/2 t baking powder
3/4 t baking soda

Frosting:
1/2 cup (1 stick) unsalted butter, softened
1 lb box confectioners sugar
4 T half and half
food coloring
sprinkles

- Cookies: In a large bowl with an electric mixer, combine butter and both sugars until light and fluffy, 3 minutes. Beat in eggs until well combined. Sift together flour, baking powder and soda and slowly add to batter until just combined. Form dough into a disk, wrap in plastic and chill 2 hours
- Preheat oven to 350°
- On a lightly floured surface, roll out dough to 1/4"thickness. Cut out shapes with a cookie cutter (make sure the cookie cutter is dipped in flour each time). Place 2" apart on parchment lined baking sheets
- Bake 10-12 minutes until golden brown. Cool on wire racks before frosting
- Frosting: Beat butter and confectioners sugar. Slowly add half and half and beat to a creamy consistency. Divide into 5 small bowls adding food coloring to four and leaving one white

- Frost cookies and add sprinkles before frosting dries

Makes approximately 4 dozen

Grammy's Christmas Cookies

When I was given this 30 year old recipe in all its originality, I never expected a whole chapter on how to bake cookies. The abridged description of the cookies is as follows: "An annual affair at our house are these really glamorous cookies!" Here are a few tips on decorating: "Give each cookie a complete color job. Have fun and let your imagination have a field day". With the recipe were the original cookie cutters that my husband, Jim used when he was a little boy. Now, when I make them with our son Jimmy, I'm reminded why family traditions are so special. By the way, these are the best sugar cookies I have ever tasted, and I bake them year around.

Cookies:
1 cup (2 sticks) unsalted butter,
softened
1 cup sugar
2 large eggs
1 T vanilla
3 cups flour
1/2 t salt

Frosting:
2 large egg whites
1/4 t cream of tartar
1/4 t vanilla
2 1/2 cups confectioners
sugar
food coloring
sprinkles

- Cookies: In a large bowl with an electric mixer, combine butter and sugar until light and fluffy. Beat in eggs and vanilla until combined. Sift together flour and salt and slowly add to batter until just combined. Form dough into a disk, wrap in plastic and chill 2 hours
- Preheat oven to 375°
- On a lightly floured surface, roll out dough to 1/4"thickness. Cut out shapes with a cookie cutter (make sure the cookie cutter is dipped in flour each time). Place 2" apart on parchment lined baking sheet
- Bake 10-12 minutes until golden brown. Cool on wire racks before frosting

- <u>Frosting</u>: Beat egg whites, vanilla and cream of tarter until foamy. Gradually beat in sugar until frosting forms peaks. Divide into 5 small bowls adding food coloring to four and leaving one white
- Frost cookies and add sprinkles before frosting dries

Makes approximately 3 dozen

Almond Apricot Biscotti

One night I was out with my friend, Christina, and on the way to dinner, she said "Oh no! I'm making biscotti and I forgot to take them out of the oven". The biscotti were having their second baking and in her rush to get out of the house, she forgot about them (Don't laugh, I do this all the time). She called home and had the babysitter turn off the oven, but they remained in there, inadvertently, overnight. The next day I asked her how they turned out, and she said they were just fine. The reason? You really can't overcook biscotti. In fact, the drier the better. I don't recommend leaving them in the oven overnight, but if you're looking for a practically foolproof cookie recipe, biscotti are a great choice.

2 cups flour
3/4 cup sugar
1 1/2 t baking powder
1/2 t salt
4 T (1/2 stick) unsalted butter, cold and cut up
1 large egg, lightly beaten
1/3 cup whole milk

1 T fresh orange juice
1/2 t vanilla
1/4 t almond extract
1 cup whole almonds. toasted
1 cup dried apricots, chopped

- Preheat oven to 350°
- In a large bowl, sift together flour, sugar, baking powder and salt. Add butter and combine with two knives or clean fingers until mixture resembles coarse crumbs. Add egg, milk, orange juice, vanilla and almond extract and stir with a fork until dough forms. Mix in almonds and apricots
- Divide dough into two 12x3" logs. Place logs on a parchment lined baking sheet
- Bake 20 minutes until lightly brown. Cool 20 minutes. Reduce oven temperature to 300°
- Transfer cooled logs to a cutting board and with a serrated knife, cut diagonally in 1/2" slices. Return to prepared sheet and bake 30 minutes until biscotti are dry
- Cool on wire racks

Makes approximately 5 1/2 dozen

White Chocolate Macadamia Nut Brownies

Sometimes making cookies can be so tedious; forming little balls and arranging them on a cookie sheet and always wondering if they're too close together. Well, you never have to worry about that with brownies. So, if you're in a rush or just don't feel like spending a lot of time in the kitchen, any type of brownie is the perfect solution to a quick, homemade dessert.

12 oz package of white chocolate chips
10 T (1 stick + 2T) unsalted butter
4 large eggs
2 cups sugar
2 t vanilla
2 cups flour
1t baking powder

1/2 t salt
1 cup macadamia nuts,
toasted and chopped

- In a double boiler, melt chocolate and butter (mixture will melt but not combine). Remove from heat and cool slightly, 30 minutes
- Preheat oven to 350°
- In a large bowl, with an electric mixer beat eggs, sugar and vanilla until light and lemony. Beat in chocolate mixture to combine. Sift together flour, baking powder and salt and slowly add to batter until just combined. Fold in nuts
- Spread into a buttered 13x9" baking pan
- Bake 35-40 minutes, until tester comes out clean
- Cool brownies completely and cut into squares

Makes 15 brownies

Loaded Blondies

Let's face it, almost any brownie or cookie can taste good if they have assorted chips and candy in them. It's along those lines that I made up this recipe. Basically, I threw in everything in the pantry and I felt like I was cheating in the most culinary way. Nevertheless, a blondie was born. I was planning on never making it again, but my discerning husband declared it a winner. So here it is.

1/2 cup (1 stick) unsalted butter, softened
1 1/2 cups packed dark brown sugar
3 large eggs
1 t vanilla
2 1/4 cups flour
2 t baking powder
1 t salt
1 cup mini marshmallows

1 cup semisweet chocolate chips
1 cup white chocolate chips
1 cup English toffee bits
18 caramels, unwrapped and chopped

- Preheat oven to 350°
- In a medium bowl, with an electric mixer beat butter and sugar until light and fluffy. Beat in eggs and vanilla until combined. Sift together flour, baking powder and salt and slowly add until just combined. Fold in half the marshmallows, chocolates, toffee chips and caramels. Spread in a buttered 13x9" baking pan. Scatter remaining candy evenly on top
- Bake 35 minutes until tester comes out clean
- Cool completely and cut into squares

Makes 15 brownies

Caramel Pecan Squares

This is one of my oldest and favorite recipes. It's a classic and will satisfy any sweet tooth. You can make these squares even sweeter by dipping them in melted chocolate. Just melt semisweet or milk chocolate in a double boiler and dip each cooled square half way in the chocolate. Place on parchment paper and chill until set. Know one will believe that you made them yourself!

Crust:
18 T (2 sticks +2 T) unsalted butter, softened
3/4 cup packed light brown sugar
3 cups flour
1/2 t salt
Filling:
1/2 cup (1 stick) unsalted butter
1/2 cup packed light brown sugar

2 T sugar
6 T honey
2 T heavy cream
1/4 t salt
1 t vanilla
2 cups pecan halves, toasted

- Preheat oven to 375°
- Crust: In a large bowl with an electric mixer, beat butter and sugar until light and fluffy. Sift together flour and salt and mix until dough looks clumpy. Press into a buttered 13x9" baking pan
- Prick all over with a fork, chill 20 minutes, then bake 20 minutes. Reduce oven temperature to 325°
- Filling: In a medium saucepan over medium/high heat, combine butter, both sugars, honey, heavy cream and salt. Bring to a boil stirring constantly for 1 minute. Remove from heat and stir in vanilla and pecans
- Pour filling over crust and bake 20 minutes
- Cool completely and cut into squares

Makes 15 squares

Butterscotch Bar Cookies

This is one of the first cookies that I made from my Nanny's repertory. They were supposed to be cut like a diamond, but I was so young when I first started baking them that I could never figure out how to get that diamond shape. When I asked Nanny, she would explain that you cut the finished cookies on a diagonal. But when I did it, all I got was a bunch of misshapen triangles. Even when we baked them together, her hand was much more precise than mine at that elusive diamond shape. So, I changed the shape to triangles. If any of you out there can cut a good diamond cookie please do so, they taste much better that way.

1 cup (2 sticks) unsalted butter, softened
1 1/2 cups packed light brown sugar
1 large egg, separated
1 t vanilla
2 cups flour
pinch salt
1/4 cup sugar
1 cup chopped pecans, toasted

- Preheat oven to 350°
- In a large bowl with an electric mixer, beat butter and brown sugar until light and fluffy. Beat in egg yolk and vanilla until combined. Sift together flour and salt and slowly add until just combined. Press dough in a buttered 13x9" baking pan
- Beat egg white until foamy and spread over dough then sprinkle sugar and pecans. Lightly press pecans into dough
- Bake 20 minutes until golden brown
- Cut immediately into squares, then triangles

Makes 36 cookies

Toffee Triangles

It's a fairly common occurrence that when my kids come home from school, they'll bring a friend home too. Just to do homework, of course. Not a play date, so they say. My son Jimmy has one friend in particular, Sam, who comes over a lot. I always offer them my latest baked goodie with a glass of milk. There are few kids who appreciate this as much as Sam. Jimmy tells me that these are Sam's favorite. They go great with milk too.

Crust:
3/4 cup (1 1/2 sticks) unsalted butter, softened
3/4 cup packed light brown sugar
1 large egg yolk
1 1/2 cups flour
1/4 t salt
1 cup chopped pecans

Filling
14 oz can sweetened, condensed milk
2 T unsalted butter
2 T vanilla
12 oz package semisweet chocolate chips

- Preheat oven to 350°
- Crust: In a large bowl with an electric mixer, beat butter and sugar until light and fluffy. Beat in egg yolk until combined. Sift together flour and salt and slowly add until just combined. Press dough in a buttered 13x9" baking pan
- Bake for 20 minutes until lightly brown. Remove from heat and set aside
- Filling: In a medium saucepan, over medium heat combine condensed milk and 2 tablespoons butter. Bring to a boil stirring constantly for 5 minutes. Turn off heat, stir in vanilla and pour over baked crust
- Bake for 15 minutes
- Sprinkle with chocolate chips and bake 2 more minutes until melted. Spread chocolate evenly then sprinkle with pecans. Cover and chill until chocolate is set
- Cut into triangles

Makes 30 triangles

<u>Peanut Chewy Bars</u>

When I was little, my mother's favorite candy was a caramel and peanut concoction covered in dark chocolate. Mom used to hide them from us kids, but we always found them in all the regular places: Her sock drawer, under the extra pillows in the guest room, behind the phone books in the kitchen. Many years later I was experimenting with a caramel bar recipe when I discovered that if I added peanuts, it would taste a lot like those chewy candy bars that I hunted for so many years ago. My biggest critic, mom, thinks they're pretty good too.

Crust:
3/4 cup (1 1/2 sticks) unsalted butter, melted
1 cup flour
1 cup old fashioned oats
3/4 cup packed light brown sugar
1 t baking soda
1/2 t salt
Filling:
12 oz bag caramels (about 32)

3 T unsalted butter
3 T heavy cream
1 cup semisweet chocolate chips
1 cup unsalted dry roasted peanuts, chopped

- Preheat oven to 350°
- <u>Crust:</u> In a medium bowl with a wooden spoon, combine butter, flour, oats, brown sugar, baking soda and salt. Press 3/4 of the mixture into a buttered 13x9" baking pan
- Bake 15 minutes until lightly brown
- <u>Filling:</u> In a small saucepan over low heat, combine the caramels, butter and cream until melted. Pour caramel mixture over the baked crust tilting the pan to make sure the crust is covered. Sprinkle evenly with chocolate chips, peanuts and remaining oatmeal mixture
- Bake 15 minutes
- Cool and cut into bars

Makes 15 bars

Fresh Raspberry Crumb Bars

Sometimes finding a good recipe is like shopping for that perfect little black dress. Black dresses are everywhere, but finding the one that's the right style and fit is the challenge. I'd been looking for the perfect raspberry bar for years. Every recipe that I came across just didn't seem right. Some had coconut, some had nuts. Most were overly complicated. Then one summer day it hit me. A basic shortbread crust with raspberry jam and fresh raspberries! It's such an obvious combination. Well, if I say so myself, it's just perfect. Now, if I could only find that black dress...

2 sticks (1 cup) unsalted butter, softened
1/2 cup confectioners sugar
2 cups flour
1/2 t salt
1 cup raspberry jam
1/2 cup old fashioned oats
6 oz container fresh raspberries

- Preheat oven to 350°
- In a large bowl, with an electric mixer, beat butter and sugar until light and fluffy. Sift together flour and salt and slowly add until just combined. Press 2/3 of the dough into a buttered 13x9" baking pan.
- Bake 10 minutes until lightly brown
- Spread raspberry jam on warm crust. Add oats to reserved dough and mix with a fork or clean fingers. Sprinkle over raspberry jam and press in a little. Sprinkle fresh raspberries on top.
- Bake 25 minutes until lightly brown
- Cool and cut into squares

Makes 15 bars

Lemon Squares

I've been going to a lot of birthday parties and I'm not talking about children's birthday parties. It's the big 4-0h! and the girls are celebrating. It's a great excuse for a girl's night out celebrating 40 years young. Whoever the birthday girl is, the plan is always the same. Half the ladies bring a hors d'oeuvres, half bring a dessert and everyone drinks champagne and has a grand old time. I'm always asked to bring the lemon squares. They're a big hit because I make them extra lemony and sour. Don't skimp on the lemon zest either.

Crust:
1 3/4 cups flour
3/4 cup (1 1/2 sticks) + 2 T unsalted
butter, cold and cut up
1/4 cup confectioners sugar
Filling:
1 1/2 cups sugar
3 large eggs

2 T grated lemon zest
2/3 cup freshly squeezed
lemon juice (5-6 lemons)
1/3 cup flour
1/2 t baking powder

- Preheat oven to 350°
- Crust: In a food processor, pulse flour, butter and confectioners sugar until mixture forms coarse crumbs. Press dough into a buttered 13x9" baking pan
- Bake 15 minutes until crust is firm but not brown
- Filling: In a medium bowl with an electric mixer, beat sugar, eggs, lemon zest, lemon juice, flour and baking powder until blended. Pour over baked crust
- Bake 25 minutes until filling is firm in center
- Cool completely. Dust with confectioners sugar and cut into squares

Makes 15 squares

Tea Brownies

I was first introduced to these brownies by my friend Ashley. We were having a potluck barbecue and this is what she brought. I was dazzled by their uniqueness. Brownies are a dime a dozen, but these managed to be traditional, yet the layer of vanilla butter cream under a topping of chocolate ganache was the type of dessert you'd expect to find in a fine restaurant. So the next time you're asked to bring a dessert to a potluck supper or any party, impress them with tea brownies.

Brownie:
4 oz unsweetened chocolate
1 cup (2 sticks) unsalted butter
4 large eggs
2 cups sugar
1 t vanilla
1 cup flour
1/2 t salt

Frosting
3 cups confectioners sugar
2 T unsalted butter, softened
1/4 cup heavy cream
ganache:
4 oz semisweet chocolate
1 T unsalted butter

- Brownie: Melt chocolate and butter in a double boiler, stirring to combine. Remove from heat and set aside to cool slightly, 30 minutes
- Preheat oven to 325°
- In a medium bowl with an electric mixer beat eggs and sugar until light and lemony. Beat in vanilla then fold in chocolate mixture to combine. Sift flour into batter slowly until just combined. Pour into a buttered 13x9" baking pan
- Bake 30 minutes until top is cracked and firm. Cool 30 minutes
- Frosting: In a medium bowl with an electric mixer, beat sugar, butter and cream until smooth (If too thick, add more heavy cream)
- Spread over cooled brownies. Chill 30 minutes
- Ganache: Melt chocolate and butter in a double boiler, stirring to combine. Cool slightly and spread over icing
- Chill 30 minutes, then cut into squares

Makes 15 brownies

Volcano Brownies

Volcano brownies are big, full bodied, very dense and full of flavor. A word of caution: If you leave these marshmallow-topped treats in the oven for even a minute too long, they will get too toasted and then you've ruined the whole batch. There's nothing more frustrating. Believe me, I've made that mistake. Keep a watchful eye those last five minutes.

6 oz unsweetened chocolate
3/4 cup (1 1/2 sticks) unsalted butter
4 large eggs
2 1/4 cups sugar
1 1/2 t instant espresso powder
1 t vanilla
1 1/3 cup flour
1/4 t salt
1 cup semisweet chocolate chunks

1 cup mini marshmallows
1 cup chopped walnuts, toasted

- Preheat oven to 350°
- Melt chocolate and butter in a double boiler, stirring to combine. Remove from heat, set aside to cool slightly, 30 minutes
- In a large bowl with an electric mixer beat eggs, sugar and espresso until light and smooth. Beat in vanilla until combined. Fold in chocolate mixture to combine. Sift together flour and salt and slowly add until just combined. Pour into buttered 13x9" baking pan
- Bake 30 minutes until top is cracked and firm
- Sprinkle chocolate, marshmallows and nuts evenly over the top. Return to oven and bake 5 minutes until marshmallows are lightly browned
- Cool and cut into squares

Makes 15 squares

Seven Layer Bars

When I was about 10, I began to feel my independence in the kitchen and started baking from real recipes. This is one of the first desserts I ever made and it's about as simple as it gets. You can certainly change the combination of toppings to your preference, but this is the one that I remember making all those years ago.

1/2 cup (1 stick) unsalted butter
1 1/2 cups graham cracker crumbs
14 oz can sweetened condensed milk
12 oz bag semisweet chocolate chips
7 oz bag sweetened coconut
12 oz bag English toffee bits
6 oz bag chopped pecans or almonds, toasted

- Preheat oven to 350°
- Place butter in a 13x9" baking pan and place in the oven until butter melts. Sprinkle graham cracker crumbs evenly over butter. Pour sweetened condensed milk over crumbs. Top with chocolate chips, coconut, toffee bits and nuts. Lightly press in with the back of a spoon
- Bake 30 minutes
- Cool and cut into bars

Makes 20 bars

Fortunate Cookies (Schneken)

When I first started working in advertising in New York City, my proud mother, unbeknownst to me, sent a batch of Schneken that I had just made to the frozen food buyer at a well known bakery. I was at work when I got the phone call declaring my schneken "the best thing he had tasted in years". I could be the next big thing, he said. But wait! I just finished college, I finally got a job and I was really enjoying it. I didn't want to be the next big thing! Well, now I do, but I guess it's too late. I'm sure you're wondering what exactly is a schneken? It's a German pastry similar to a rugula. It's the first thing I ever made with my Nanny. To this day I bring them to my grandfather whenever I see him. He likes them with extra jelly so they ooze out the sides creating a chewy edge. By the way, I call them fortunate cookies because you're fortunate to have this wonderful cookie.

1 cup (2 sticks) unsalted butter, softened
8 oz package of cream cheese, softened
2 cups flour
8 oz jar raspberry or apricot preserves

1 cup raisins
1 cup sugar
2 T cinnamon

- In a large bowl with an electric mixer beat butter and cream cheese until smooth. Sift flour slowly into mixture until just combined
- Turn dough out on a floured work surface and divide into six equal balls. Wrap individually in plastic and chill 2 hours
- Preheat oven to 350°
- On a lightly floured surface, roll first ball to 9" in diameter. Divide into 8 slices like a pizza
- Spread 1 teaspoon of jam on each slice then 1 teaspoon of raisins. Roll each slice from large end to small, to form a crescent
- In a small bowl combine sugar and cinnamon. Roll each cookie in sugar mixture and place on parchment lined baking sheets
- Bake 20-25 minutes until golden brown
- Cool on wire racks

Makes 48 cookies

Desserts - Cakes and Pies

Sour Cream Chocolate Cake

This is a special dessert in the Currie household. It's the only cake my husband, Jim, has ever had on his birthday. That's right, his mom made it for him when he was growing up and passed the recipe to me when we got married. It is now the official birthday cake for everyone in our family.

Cake:
1/4 cup (1/2 stick) unsalted butter
4 oz unsweetened chocolate
2 cups sugar
2 large eggs
1 t vanilla
1 cup water
3/4 cup sour cream
2 cups flour
1 1/4 t baking soda

1/2 t baking powder
1/2 t salt
Frosting:
1/2 cup (1 stick) unsalted butter
4 oz unsweetened chocolate
1 lb box confectioners sugar
1 cup sour cream
2 t vanilla

- Cake: In a double boiler, melt butter and chocolate, stirring often. Remove from heat and set aside to cool slightly, 30 minutes
- Preheat oven to 350°
- Butter and flour 2, 9" round baking pans
- In a large bowl with and electric mixer, beat sugar and eggs, until light and lemony. Beat in vanilla, water, sour cream and chocolate mixture until combined. Sift together flour, baking soda and powder and salt and slowly add until just combined
- Pour into prepared pans and bake 25-30 minutes, until tester comes out clean
- Cool on wire racks
- Frosting: In a double boiler, melt butter and chocolate, stirring often. Remove from heat and set aside to cool slightly, 30 minutes
- In a large bowl with an electric mixer beat confectioners sugar, sour cream and vanilla until smooth. Add chocolate mixture and beat until combined
- Spread on cooled cake

Serves 8-10

Chocolate Mousse Cake

What could be easier than a rich, indulgent cake with only three ingredients? Whenever I serve it, people can't believe the utter simplicity. But there's a catch. The success of this cake requires time, patience, and precision. Combine your finesse with the freshest ingredients and you'll be thrilled with the results.

1 lb bittersweet chocolate
1 cup (2 sticks) unsalted butter
8 large eggs, room temperature

- Melt butter and chocolate in a double boiler, stirring often. Remove from heat and set aside to cool to room temperature, one hour
- Preheat oven to 350°
- Line the bottom of an 8" spring form pan with parchment paper, then butter the paper and sides of the pan. Place pan on a sheet of aluminum foil and mold the foil on the bottom and around the sides, but not on the top
- In a large bowl whisk the eggs until combined. Slowly whisk in the cooled chocolate mixture. Pour batter into prepared pan, place pan in shallow baking pan and place in oven. Pour 1" of hot water in the shallow pan
- Bake 45 minutes until edges are set, but center is still loose
- Remove from oven and remove spring form pan from water. Cover and chill overnight
- To serve, remove spring form pan sides
- Invert cake onto a cookie sheet, remove parchment and re-invert onto a serving platter
- Dust with confectioners sugar

Serves 10-12

Flourless Chocolate Cake

I have to admit, I'm a holiday hog. Our families live all over now, so when we can get together, it's special. There's only one problem: Everyone expects the same exact meal every Thanksgiving, Christmas and Easter. One dessert that I always make for all three holidays is flourless chocolate cake. It's easy, I can make it in advance, and it always turns out delicious. This recipe also travels well, so if you need to bring a dessert to someone's house, this is a winning choice.

1 1/3 cups sugar
1 cup (2 sticks) unsalted butter
6 oz semisweet chocolate

6 oz unsweetened chocolate
5 large eggs, room temperature

- In a small saucepan, bring 1 cup sugar with 1/2 cup water to a boil, stirring to dissolve sugar. Boil the syrup without stirring for 4 minutes then cool to room temperature, 1 hour
- In a double boiler, melt butter and both chocolates, stirring often. Remove from heat and set aside to cool to room temperature, 1 hour
- Preheat oven to 350°
- Butter a 9" round cake pan. Line the pan bottom with parchment paper and butter the paper. Dust the pan with flour
- In a large bowl with an electric mixer, beat eggs with remaining 1/3 cup sugar at high speed for 10 minutes until mixture has tripled in volume. Slowly pour in cooled sugar syrup, beating to combine. With a rubber spatula, fold in chocolate mixture until blended
- Pour batter into prepared pan, place pan in shallow baking pan and place in the oven. Pour 1" of hot water in the shallow pan
- Bake 1 hour and 15 minutes. Cake will be very moist with a slight crust on top
- Remove from oven and remove cake from water. Cover and chill overnight

- To serve, run a warm knife around edge to loosen cake. Gently heat the pan bottom by placing it in hot water for 1-2 minutes. Invert cake onto a cookie sheet. Remove parchment and re-invert onto a serving platter
- Dust with confectioner's sugar.

Serves 10-12

Fancy Chocolate Pudding

This recipe has a split personality. Homemade chocolate pudding is a child's dream. But, it's a favorite of mine for a dinner party. It can be made ahead of time and chilled in the refrigerator up to one day before serving. Just add a little whipped cream and some sliced berries and you have one terrific dessert.

1 cup heavy cream
1 cup whole milk
2 oz milk chocolate
2 oz semisweet chocolate
5 large egg yolks
1/3 cup sugar

1/4 t salt
2 t vanilla
whipped cream and berries
for serving

- Preheat oven to 325°
- In a medium saucepan,over medium heat combine cream, milk and chocolate
- Bring almost to a simmer then remove from heat, stirring until chocolate is melted. Set aside
- In a medium bowl, whisk egg yolks, sugar and salt. Slowly add the hot milk mixture to combine, whisking constantly. Whisk in vanilla
- Pour in a 9" quiche pan, then place in a shallow baking pan, then in the oven. Pour 1" of hot water in the shallow baking pan around the quiche pan
- Bake 35 minutes until pudding is set
- Remove from oven and remove pan from water
- Cool on wire rack, then chill 2 hours to overnight
- Serve with whipped cream and fresh berries

Serves 8-10

Peanut Butter Layer Cake with Milk Chocolate Frosting

When my twins were entering kindergarten, I had a little party just before school started for all the kids in their new class. I thought it would be a good opportunity for everyone, parents and children, to get to know each other before entering the world of higher learning. The sprinkler was flowing and the tunes were blaring. Lunch was easy; hamburgers and hot dogs on the grill. Dessert was a challenge. I could have served ice pops, but this was a celebration. It had to be special. The peanut butter cake was a huge hit among parents and kids alike. The combination is so childishly alluring, yet the presentation is grown up and sophisticated. Every adult is a kid at heart when it comes to this cake.

Cake:
1 cup (2 sticks) unsalted butter, softened
2 cups sugar
4 large eggs
3/4 cup smooth peanut butter
1 t vanilla
1 cup whole milk
3 cups flour

1 T baking powder
1/2 t salt
Frosting:
6 T heavy cream
4 oz milk chocolate, chopped
3/4 cup (1 1/2 sticks) unsalted butter, softened
3 cups confectioners sugar

- Cake: Preheat oven to 350°
- Butter and flour 2, 9" cake pans
- In a large bowl with an electric mixer, beat together butter and sugar until light and fluffy. Beat in eggs, peanut butter, vanilla and milk until combined. Sift together flour, baking powder and salt and slowly add until just combined
- Pour into prepared pans and bake 35-40 minutes until tester comes out clean
- Cool 10 minutes in pans then turn out onto wire racks to cool completely
- Frosting: In a small saucepan, bring cream to a boil. Pour over chocolate in a small bowl. Cool slightly, 30 minutes

- In a large bowl with an electric mixer, beat butter and sugar until light and fluffy. Beat in cooled chocolate mixture until well combined
- Spread on cake

Serves 8-10

Carrot Cake

For the most part, I like my cakes simple. Most carrot cakes have so much "junk" in them like nuts, coconut, and raisins. You name it, it can get lost in a carrot cake. This one, however, is very plain, which is why it tastes so good. It's moist, light, and smooth. Carrots should be king in a carrot cake and they are here. The frosting is lick the bowl good with the addition of lemon zest. Your guests will ask you what Makesthis cake so delicious, and you simply reply, "Oh, it's nothing, really". You won't be lying.

Cake
4 large eggs
2 cups sugar
1 1/2 cups canola oil
2 cups flour
2 t baking powder
1 1/2 t baking soda
1 t salt
2 t cinnamon
2 cups carrots (about 3), peeled and grated

8 1/2 oz can crushed pineapple, drained
Frosting
1/2 cup (1 stick) unsalted butter, softened
8 oz package cream cheese, softened
1 T vanilla
1 lb box confectioners sugar
zest from 1 lemon

- Cake: Preheat oven 350°
- Butter and flour 2, 9" cake pans
- In large bowl, whisk eggs. Whisk in sugar and oil. Sift together flour, baking powder and soda, salt and cinnamon and slowly add until just combined. Fold in carrots and pineapple
- Pour into prepared pans and bake 35-40 minutes, until tester comes out clean
- Cool in pan for 10 minutes then invert onto wire racks to cool completely
- Frosting: In a large bowl with an electric mixer, beat all ingredients to a smooth consistency
- Spread on cooled cake

Serves 8-10

Fresh Raspberry Cake

In the summertime, there's nothing like enjoying ripe fruit at its peak. I try to use as much fruit as I can in all of my baking. This raspberry cake defines the word summer to me. It originated as a dessert after dinner, but because it's not too sweet, it's terrific any time of day, even with breakfast.

12 T (1 1/2 sticks) unsalted butter, softened
1 cup sugar
2 large eggs
1 t vanilla
1/4 cup fresh orange juice
1/2 cup Marsala wine
1 t lemon zest
1 1/2 cups flour

1 t baking powder
1/4 t baking soda
1 t salt
1/4 t nutmeg
2 cups fresh raspberries

- Preheat oven to 375°
- In a large bowl with an electric mixer, beat butter and sugar until light and fluffy. Beat in eggs, vanilla, orange juice, Marsala and lemon zest until combined. Whisk together flour, baking powder, baking soda, salt, and nutmeg and slowly add until just combined
- Pour batter into a buttered 10" spring form pan. Top with 2 cups raspberries
- Bake 30-45 minutes until tester comes out clean
- Cool in pan

Serves 6-8

Pear Upside Down Cake

If raspberry cake defines summer, pear upside down cake defines fall. When the pears are really ripe, the combination with the caramelized top and the moist cake make a perfect ending to a perfect fall dinner.

Pears:
1 1/2 cups sugar
3 cups water
3 firm, ripe pears,
peeled, halved and cored

Caramel:
1/4 cup unsalted butter, softened
3/4 cup sugar
1 1/4 t baking powder
1/4 t salt

Cake:
1/2 cup (1 stick) unsalted
butter, softened
1/2 cup sugar
1/2 t vanilla
2 large eggs
3 large egg yolks
1/3 cup flour
1/3 cup white cornmeal

- Pears: In a large saucepan over high heat, bring sugar and water to a boil. Add pears to syrup. Reduce heat to low and simmer 15-20 minutes until tender, turning once
- Remove pears from syrup and drain on paper towels. Discard syrup
- Caramel: In a small saucepan over medium/high heat, combine butter and sugar to make caramel (mixture will go through several stages before turning into caramel. First it will look crystallized, then, as it smoothes out, it will look separated. Continue to cook until caramel reaches a rich golden brown color. Swirl pan if necessary to combine mixture)
- Remove from heat and pour into a 9" round cake pan. Place pear halves core side up in a circle over caramel. Set aside
- Preheat oven to 375°
- Cake: In a large bowl with an electric mixer, beat butter and sugar until light and fluffy. Beat in vanilla, eggs and egg yolks until combined. Sift together flour, corn meal, baking powder and salt and slowly add until just combined

228

- Spread batter over pears and bake 30 minutes until tester comes out clean
- Immediately run a small knife around edge to loosen. Then, carefully turn cake upside down onto serving plate
- Wait one minute before removing pan

Serves 6-8

La Galette Des Rois

My friend Sylvie is from Provence and knows a lot about food. When she goes home to visit her family, she always brings me back an epicurean surprise. Once it was fleur de sel, another time, a local cookbook. She never falls short in educating me on real French cooking, which is the best gift of all. One rainy afternoon, we were having tea at her house when out of the oven came this traditional French pastry. Translated, La Galette Des Rois means kings' cake celebrating Epiphany, or Twelfth Night, the day the three kings visited the infant Jesus. Before baking, a little toy or dried bean is snuck in. When the cake is served, the one lucky enough to get the toy has good luck. Well, I did not get the toy, but I felt lucky enjoying this delicious cake. Sylvie got the recipe from her son's kindergarten teacher when they lived in France. She tells me what Makesher galette "superior" to others are the freshly ground almonds. I couldn't agree more.

1/4 cup (1/2 stick) unsalted butter, softened
4 T sugar
1/2 cup (2 oz) freshly ground blanched almonds
1 large egg
17.3 oz package puff pastry (2 sheets)
1 ceramic "toy"
1 large egg yolk
1 t whole milk

- Preheat oven to 350°
- In a large bowl with an electric mixer, beat butter and sugar until light and fluffy. Beat in ground almonds and egg to combine. Set aside
- Place one square of puff pastry in a 9" pie plate. Place the almond filling evenly in the center. Add "toy." Place the second puff pastry sheet on top
- In a small bowl, whisk egg yolk and milk. Brush edges of pastry and "glue" together, tucking the top into the bottom and tucking the bottom around the sides. Brush top with egg wash

- Bake 30 minutes, until golden brown and puffy

Serves 6-8

Cranberry Caramel Nut Tart

Growing up, I spent every Thanksgiving at my Aunt Barbara and Uncle Bobby's house. Since this was the holiday of giving thanks, I decided at a very young age to always bring a dessert. When I think of the concoctions and outright disasters I presented year after year, I cringe. But I never knew it then because everyone was always complementary (actually, I do remember Uncle Bobby laughing at my pecan pie when he cut into it and it was all liquid). Several years ago, I wanted to bring something unique yet traditional. I brought this cranberry caramel nut tart and if I say so myself, it got rave reviews.

Pastry:
1 cup flour
1 T sugar
1/4 t salt
1/2 cup (1 stick) unsalted butter, softened
1 t vanilla
2 t ice water
Filling:
1 cup sugar
3 T light corn syrup

1/2 cup (1 stick) unsalted butter, softened
1/2 cup heavy cream
3/4 cup chopped pecans, toasted
3/4 cup chopped almonds, toasted
3/4 cup dried cranberries
2 oz bittersweet chocolate chopped

- Pastry: In a food processor combine flour, sugar and salt. Add butter and vanilla and pulse until dough resembles coarse crumbs. Add water in a steady stream and pulse until dough holds its shape
- Turn out onto lightly floured surface and press together to form a disc. Place disc in a 9" tart pan with a removable bottom pressing evenly on bottom and up sides. Place in freezer 30 minutes.
- Preheat oven to 375°
- Prick crust with a fork and bake 30-35 minutes until golden brown. Remove from oven and cool
- Filling: In a medium saucepan over medium/high heat, bring sugar and corn syrup to a boil. As sugar melts, swirl it to combine—do not stir (mixture will begin to caramelize but, if it starts to burn, remove from heat). When mixture is a rich golden

232

brown, remove from heat. Add butter and cream and stir until butter is melted. Stir in nuts and cranberries
- Pour into baked crust then sprinkle chocolate. Refrigerate 2 hours until set
- Serve chilled

Serves 8-10

Old Fashioned Blueberry Pie

A few summers ago, I was obsessed with making pie. There is an art to perfect pie crust, and the trick is lots of practice. Everyone has a different method. I like to put everything in the food processor and pulse until just combined. Then add the water, which is tricky. Too much and the dough is gluey and sloppy. Too little and it's dry and crumbly. There is no science to it, just a feeling that the water amount is just right. To complicate matters more, every pie crust turns out differently, even if the ingredients are the same. The good thing is that even if you think it looks terrible going in to the oven, chances are it will look great coming out. If you keep the filling simple, like this blueberry pie, it will taste great too.

Pie Crust:
2 1/2 cups flour
2 t sugar
1 t salt
1 cup (2 sticks) unsalted butter,
cold and cut into pieces
4-5 T ice water
milk and sugar for crust

Filling:
4 cups (2 pints) blueberries
1/2 cup sugar
1/4 cup flour
1 T fresh lemon juice
1/2 t cinnamon

- Crust: In a food processor mix flour, sugar and salt. Add butter and pulse until mixture resembles coarse crumbs. Add tablespoons of ice water one at a time and pulse to form dough
- Turn dough out onto a lightly floured surface and knead a few times. Divide into 2 discs, 1 slightly larger. Wrap smaller disc in plastic and chill 30 minutes. Roll out larger disc on a lightly floured surface to place in a 9" pie plate. Chill 30 minutes
- Preheat oven to 375°
- Filling: In a large bowl combine berries, sugar, flour, lemon juice and cinnamon. Pour filling in crust
- Roll smaller disc to fit over top, crimping the edge. Make a few slits on top, brush with milk and sprinkle with sugar
- Bake 1 hour until bubbly and crust is golden brown

Serves 6-8

Traditional Apple Pie

Every fall, the local farms become all things apple. At the stroke of
Labor Day, they turn their tractors to hayrides and open their apple
orchards to local families. The excursion begins with a comfy seat on
big blocks of hay piled high on a flatbed pulled by a tractor coughing
and sputtering exhaust fumes as it inches through the farm. Most of the
good apples are at the tops of the trees and out of reach. One by one,
the kids get a turn on daddy's shoulders. I've taken years of pictures of
our grinning children claiming their apple, with Jim grinning and
bearing it. In the end, we bring home about 25 pounds of apples. The
reward for all this hard work is a freshly baked apple pie.

9" double pie crust (page 237)
3 1/2 lbs (about 8) apples,
peeled, cored and sliced
1/2 cup sugar
2 T flour
1 t cinnamon
1/4 t nutmeg
1/4 t salt
1 T fresh lemon juice

2 T cold, unsalted butter, cut
into pieces
milk and sugar for crust

Follow directions for pie crust
- Preheat oven to 375°
- In a large bowl, toss apples, sugar, flour, cinnamon, nutmeg, salt
  and lemon juice
- Pour filling into crust and dot with butter
- Roll out smaller pie crust to fit over top, crimping the edge. Make
  a few slits on top, brush with milk and sprinkle with sugar
- Bake 1 hour until bubbly and crust is golden brown

Serves 6-8

Apple Dumplings

Several years ago Jim's whole family visited his Aunt Doreen and Uncle Don outside of Pittsburgh where we planned to attend a local fair with our young children. When we got there, to our surprise, we learned it was an antique fair. Most of the stores had big signs NO KIDS ALLOWED. While everyone else had a lovely afternoon antiquing, what saved us were the homemade apple dumplings sold on every street corner. Apparently, this Pennsylvania Dutch treat is very common in the area. When I told Aunt Doreen about our delicious discovery, she said she grew up eating her grandmother's famous apple dumplings. You guessed it, I had to have the recipe.

Syrup
1 1/2 cups sugar
1 1/2 cups water
1/4 t cinnamon
1/4 t nutmeg
3 T unsalted butter
Pastry
2 cups flour
2 t baking powder

1 t salt
2/3 cup shortening
1/2 cup whole milk
6 medium, whole apples,
peeled and cored
1/2 cup sugar
1/2 t cinnamon
4 T (1/2 stick) unsalted
butter, cut up

- Preheat oven to 375°
- Syrup: In a medium saucepan bring sugar, water, cinnamon, and nutmeg to a boil. Remove from heat and add butter. Stir until butter melts and set aside
- Pastry: In a large bowl sift together flour, baking powder and salt. Cut in shortening until mixture resembles coarse crumbs. Add milk all at once and stir until dough is formed
- On a lightly floured surface, roll dough to an 18x12" rectangle. Cut into 6, 6" squares
- Place an apple on each square and sprinkle evenly with sugar and cinnamon then dot with butter. Moisten edges of pastry, bring corners together around apple and pinch to seal
- Place 1" apart in a 13x9" baking pan. Pour syrup over dumplings

- Bake for 35 minutes until apples are tender and crust is golden brown
- Serve warm with ice cream

Serves 6

Apple Crisp

If you take a random poll of the entire extended Currie family of a favorite dessert, there's a good chance most everyone will answer grandma Currie's apple crisp. I've eaten a lot of apple crisps' and whether homemade, out of a box, or in a restaurant, I have to agree grandma Currie was onto something. It's simple and straightforward allowing the fresh apples to take center stage. One more thing about grandma Currie, She served her apple crisp warm with vanilla ice cream on top. While it's not necessary, if you're serving it to a Currie, you better not forget it.

3 1/2 lbs apples (about 8),
peeled, cored and sliced
2 T sugar
juice and zest from 1 lemon
3/4 cup packed light brown sugar
1 cup old fashioned oats

1/4 cup flour
1 t cinnamon
1/2 cup (1 stick) unsalted
butter, cut into pieces

- Preheat oven to 375°
- Toss apples with sugar, lemon juice and zest and place in a 13x9" baking dish
- In a medium bowl, combine light brown sugar, oats, flour and cinnamon. With two knives or clean fingers cut in butter until mixture forms moist clumps. Sprinkle over apples
- Bake 45 minutes until brown and bubbly
- Serve with vanilla ice cream

Serves 8-10

238

Banana Boats

I grew up going to summer camp in Maine. Once a week we had
cookouts deep in the woods. Each bunk would pick up a large wicker
basket filled with recipes and ingredients and we'd hike to a campsite to
begin cooking. Dessert was usually s'mores except once in a while we'd
be surprised with banana boats. It was a cause for celebration because
they were delectable and definitely the best part of cooking out. But
you don't have to be a camper to make this at home. I make it as a
special treat for my kids right in the oven.

4 ripe bananas
1/2 of a 10.5 oz bag of mini marshmallows
4 oz milk chocolate bar
broken into pieces
4 sheets aluminum foil

- Preheat oven to 400° or heat grill on medium/high heat
- Using a sharp knife, make a slit lengthwise down each banana
  slicing through the peel and the banana
- Loosen peel and stuff each banana with marshmallows and 1 oz
  chocolate. Press peel together to enclose filling then wrap
  bananas in foil
- Cook in oven or on grill about 7 minutes until bananas are warm,
  chocolate is melted and marshmallows are gooey
- Cool slightly before removing foil

Serves 4

<u>Goodies</u>

Spicy Pecans

I get more mileage out of this recipe than anything else. Let me explain.
First, if you're setting up a bar for a party, you need a dish of spicy
pecans. Second, if you want to jazz up your salad, just sprinkle on some
spicy pecans. Third, if you want your hostess to love you, just present
her with spicy pecans. Fourth, if you need to bribe your child's teacher,
just give them some spicy pecans (Just kidding!). They do make a nice
teachers gift, though.

2 large egg whites
1 T cayenne pepper
1 t paprika
1/2 cup sugar
1 T coarse salt
1 lb whole pecans (about 4 cups)

- Preheat oven to 300°
- In a medium bowl, beat egg whites with a wire whisk until foamy.
  Whisk in cayenne, paprika, sugar and salt. Add pecans and gently
  turn to coat
- Divide between two parchment lined rimmed baking sheets,
  spreading evenly
- Bake 30 minutes
- Remove pecans from baking sheets and immediately spread on
  new parchment paper in a single layer
- Cool completely, then serve or store in an airtight container

Makes 1 lb

Rosemary Scented Mixed Nuts

When I have a party, I love serving these addicting nuts. Each type of
nut has a different relationship with the rosemary and spices making it
hard to eat just one…or two. They also make a great hostess gift.
However, if you do give them as gifts, make sure you use at least 1/2 lb
of nuts. Anything less is skimpy.

2 lbs unsalted mixed nuts
1 T unsalted butter, melted
3 T fresh rosemary, chopped
1 T packed dark brown sugar
1 T salt
1/2 t cayenne pepper

- Preheat oven to 350°
- Place nuts in a rimmed baking sheet. Pour butter over and toss
- Bake until fragrant and toasted, 15 minutes
- In a medium bowl, combine rosemary, brown sugar, salt and
  cayenne
- Toss nuts in mixture while still warm

Makes 2 lbs

Tamari Sunflower Seeds

I have a little obsession with salty snacks. Whenever I'm in a different part of the country I like to go into a supermarket to see what flavor potato chips they have. On the home front, I'm always cooking up new ways to have a snack. This is great to serve at a party near the bar or as an easy snack. Tamari is flavorful soy sauce and it Makesbeautiful music with toasted sunflower seeds.

1 cup (5.5oz) dry roasted, unsalted sunflower seeds (shelled)
2 T tamari (soy sauce)

- Preheat oven to 400°
- Place sunflower seeds on a rimmed baking sheet. Bake 8 minutes until fragrant. Toss with tamari while warm
- Place in oven 2 more minutes to dry seeds

Makes 1 cup

Blue Cheese and Almond Stuffed Olives

My husband, Jim loves martinis. Sometimes I wonder if it's the actual martini that he loves or the olives. Not too long ago he read about a bar that served martinis with blue cheese olives. Jim doesn't request a lot, so when he asked me to make the olives, I was happy to go to work. I actually could hardly call it a recipe, but Jim was thrilled. Though it's not my cocktail of choice, I was told on good authority that is was perfect.

1 jar (about 5 oz) large green olives, pitted
1/2 cup blue cheese
1/2 cup whole almonds, toasted

- Drain olives reserving liquid in jar (If olives have pimentos, remove and discard)
- Place 1/2 teaspoon of blue cheese in each olive (do not over stuff or olive will split apart). Plug up hole with one almond
- Serve in a bowl or in a martini
- Place leftovers back in jar with olive juice. Store for 1 week

Makes approximately 1 cup

Crunchy After School Snack

I was at our swim club one day when my friend, Gloria, came over and offered me this warm snack mix just out of the oven. It smelled amazing as I eagerly dug in. I had to have the recipe. Gloria said she made it all the time as she rattled off the ingredients. With that she snapped the lid shut and went swimming. She told me to help myself, but I didn't want to be a pig. So I sat there, by myself, thinking about how much I wanted to eat the entire container. I started sneaking it, a little at a time. I literally had to move to another chair to stop eating it. Now, I make this snack all the time. My kids especially love it after school, which Makesme happy because it's a healthier alternative to chips.

1 cup canola oil
1 T dry dill
1 T garlic powder
1 oz package dry ranch-seasoning mix
8 cups Crispix cereal
2 cups oyster crackers

- Preheat oven to 425°
- In a large bowl, whisk oil, dill, garlic powder and ranch seasoning. Gently mix in Crispix and oyster crackers
- Pour in a 13x9" baking dish
- Bake for 20 minutes, tossing after 10 minutes

Makes approximately 12 cups

Perfect Party Mix

Nothing is better than this mix if you're having a kids party or as a teacher gift or even a hostess gift. As the seasons and holidays change, you change the colors of the M&M's. In case you didn't know (as I didn't), they come in seasonal colors: black and orange for Halloween, red and green for Christmas, red, white and blue for Fourth of July, etc. It Makesa great statement and you always have that perfect treat when you need it.

2/3 cup sugar
1/2 cup (1 stick) unsalted butter
2/3 cup sugar
1/4 cup corn syrup
1 t vanilla
8.7 oz package pretzel Goldfish
4 cups Crispix cereal
1 cup dry roasted peanuts
14 oz package M&M's

- Preheat oven to 250°
- In a small saucepan melt butter, sugar and corn syrup. Bring to a boil then reduce to a simmer and cook 5 minutes, stirring often. Turn off heat and stir in vanilla
- Place pretzels, Crispix and peanuts in a large rimmed baking sheet. Pour hot mixture over and gently stir to combine
- Bake 20 minutes, toss then add M&M's, toss again and bake 5 more minutes
- Cool on parchment paper until no longer sticky

Makes approximately 10 cups

Caramel Corn

Every Halloween, my kids come home with bulging bags of candy. Like most parents, when they aren't looking, I dig through the bags to take out my favorites. There's one thing that we all fight over. It's the homemade caramel popcorn balls that one of my neighbors makes. I know they're safe because I've been eating them since the twins started trick or treating so many years ago. Back then they could care less about a popcorn ball. Now, it's one of their favorites. I decided there was no need to wait for Halloween to have homemade caramel corn, so I started to make it myself. Now, there is plenty for everyone.

4 T (1/2 stick) unsalted butter
1/3 cup sugar
2 T light corn syrup
1/2 t vanilla
3 oz bag 94% light microwave popcorn, popped (10 cups)

- In a medium saucepan fitted with a candy thermometer, combine butter, sugar and corn syrup. Bring to a boil, stirring constantly until mixture reaches 280°, about 10 minutes
- Remove from heat and stir in vanilla
- In a large bowl, slowly pour caramel over popcorn and gently toss (caramel will be hot!)
- Cool until no longer sticky

Makes 10 cups

Chunky Crunchy Chocolates

Whenever I entertain, I love serving little unexpected extras. They especially make a statement if they're homemade. This is an easy recipe that looks and tastes great on a little silver serving plate, and I like to pull them out after dessert and coffee. If you prefer, you can substitute or omit the nuts and fruit to your personal taste. However, the color combination of the cherries, apricots, pistachios and cashews make a beautiful presentation against the dark chocolate.

1 1/4 lbs semisweet chocolate
2/3 cup dried cherries
2/3 cup dried apricots, chopped
2/3 cup salted pistachios, chopped
2/3 cup salted dry roasted cashews, chopped

- Line an 8" square baking pan with non-stick aluminum foil leaving a 2" overhang.
- Melt chocolate in a double boiler until smooth
- Remove chocolate from heat and stir in fruit and nuts. Spread evenly in pan
- Chill until firm, 1 hour
- Lift candy out of pan using the overhanging foil. Peel off foil and cut into small squares

Makes 36 pieces

Chocolate Crisps

When it comes to cooking and discovering new recipes, my mother-in-law, Dottie, is one of my biggest supporters. So, when she called me about a new one, I couldn't wait to try it. My daughter, Catie, and I were hosting our mother-daughter book club the following week and the book we selected was all about a boy who gets chocolate fever. Catie thought this would be perfect to serve and I knew I would get honest feedback on the recipe. Together, Catie and I made the chocolate crisps, and they were such a success we couldn't get the girls to sit down and discuss the book. Catie suspected the crisps gave everyone chocolate fever!

12 oz package semisweet chocolate chips
2 cups Rice Krispies
2 cups graham cracker crumbs

- In a double boiler, melt chocolate chips. Remove from heat and pour into a large bowl. Stir in Rice Krispies and graham cracker crumbs. Mix well
- Place mounded tablespoons on parchment lined baking sheets. Press with the back of a spoon to flatten slightly
- Chill until chocolate is set

Makes 24-30 crisps

English Toffee Grahams

This is a very child friendly recipe. When I'm bringing a treat into the classroom, this one comes to mind first. My kids love to help me make it, from arranging the graham crackers to sprinkling the chocolate chips to breaking apart the finished product. It also Makesa great teacher's gift. Getting the kids involved helps them understand the value of appreciation and the art of saying thank you.

12 large graham crackers
3/4 cup (1 1/2 sticks) unsalted butter
1/2 cup packed light brown sugar
1/8 t salt
12 oz package semisweet chocolate chips
1 cup chopped pecans, toasted

- Preheat oven to 375°
- Line a 15x10" rimmed baking sheet with non-stick aluminum foil
- Place graham crackers in a single layer on the baking sheet
- In a small saucepan heat butter, brown sugar and salt until melted and combined. Pour over graham crackers spreading evenly
- Bake 10 minutes until bubbly
- Remove from oven and sprinkle chocolate chips over crackers. Bake another minute until chips are melted, then spread evenly. Sprinkle pecans over chocolate and chill until chocolate is set
- Break into pieces

Makes approximately 2 lbs

English Toffee

In many ways my neighborhood is a throwback to the 50's. Our door is always open and the neighborhood kids run from house to house like free spirits making the most wonderful childhood memories. We have all kinds of neighborhood traditions like a Halloween parade, an Easter egg hunt, and the block party. But I think my favorite is the exchange of gifts among neighbors during the holidays in December. Our family gives English toffee and I begin making it just after Thanksgiving. After making many batches of this buttery confection I learned if you watch your candy thermometer closely, it will turn out perfectly. When it's finished, you won't believe you made something this good.

1 cup (2 sticks) unsalted butter
1 1/2 cups sugar
1/8 t salt
3 T light corn syrup
2 cups chopped almonds, toasted
12 oz package semisweet or milk chocolate, melted and cooled

- In a small saucepan fitted with a candy thermometer, heat butter, sugar, salt, corn syrup and 3 tablespoons water. Cook, stirring occasionally until the candy thermometer reaches 300°
- Remove from heat and stir in 1 cup chopped almonds
- Spread on a buttered large rimmed baking sheet. Spread half the chocolate, then sprinkle half the nuts over candy mixture
- Flip onto a buttered large cookie sheet. Spread remaining chocolate and sprinkle remaining nuts
- Chill until chocolate is set
- Break into pieces

Makes approximately 3 lbs

Cinnamon Spice Peanut Brittle

My mom has a secret. In her nightstand in the bottom drawer is her candy supply. I first discovered it when I was about 6. Her drawer had all of my favorites, licorice, gum drops, milk chocolate, and peanut brittle, to name a few. I couldn't take too much because it would blow my cover. Today she still has that candy drawer and when I visit, we enjoy it together. After all those years, I thought it only fair to make her something homemade. Now, my cinnamon spice peanut brittle is along side the gummy candy and the peanut chewys.

1/2 cup water
2 cups sugar
1/4 t cream of tartar
1 cup light corn syrup
2 t cinnamon
1/2 t nutmeg
2 T unsalted butter
2 cups salted peanuts
1 t baking soda

- In a medium saucepan fitted with a candy thermometer, combine water, sugar, cream of tartar and corn syrup. Bring to a boil stirring occasionally until mixture reaches 340°. The color will be golden brown
- Remove from heat and stir in cinnamon, nutmeg, butter, peanuts and baking soda, one at a time in that order
- Pour mixture onto a rimmed baking sheet lined with non-stick aluminum foil. Chill until firm, then break into pieces

Makes approximately 2 lbs

Peppermint Bark

When my brother JB and his wife Aimee moved into their first house, they decided to paint the entire place themselves. When JB called to tell me they wouldn't be able to come for Christmas due to the painting, I completely understood. Then, a few days before, JB called me asking if I was making peppermint bark. If I was, maybe they would come after all. I said no need to drive 2 hours for the peppermint bark, I'll mail it to you. They spent Christmas day painting their new abode, munching on my homemade confection. Once they got settled, they came for a visit and we enjoyed some more.

2 lbs white chocolate
12 full size candy canes
1/2 t peppermint extract

- In a double boiler melt chocolate, stirring occasionally
- Meanwhile place candy canes in a plastic bag and crush into 1/4" pieces with the back of a big spoon or a rolling pin
- Stir chopped candy cane and peppermint extract into melted chocolate
- Remove from heat and pour into a large, rimmed baking sheet lined with parchment paper
- Chill until firm, then break into pieces

Makes approximately 2 1/2lbs

Caramel Fudge Sauce

My sister—in-law, Christy, and her husband Michael have a gift of making the most ordinary event outrageously fun. Recently, after a family dinner at their home, they showcased a fabulous dessert. One by one, they brought out bowls of chocolate chips, granola, marshmallows, nuts, maraschino cherries, you name it. If you could put it on ice cream, they had it. Then came the sauces: Caramel, hot fudge and strawberry, followed by freshly made whipped cream and finally the vanilla ice cream. Our kids built their own sundae then happily retreated to their table. Make your own sundaes are a great ending to a dinner party but, it doesn't have to be an elaborate extravaganza a la Christy and Michael. This caramel chocolate sauce is simply perfect over a bowl of ice cream.

30 caramels
1 cup semisweet chocolate chips
5 oz can evaporated milk
1/2cup (1 stick) unsalted butter, cut up

- In a 1 quart microwave safe bowl, combine caramels, chocolate chips, milk and butter. Cover with plastic wrap punched with holes to let steam escape
- Microwave on high for 2 minutes. Stir and microwave 1-2 minutes longer until the caramels are almost melted
- Stir until smooth then cool for 30 minutes, stirring often
- Serve over ice cream

Makes 2 cups

Pink Applesauce

My kids could eat this every day, but I save it for special occasions. You're probably thinking holiday, but that's not it. I save it for sick days. It works like a charm. When they're lying in bed feeling blue, I make a batch of pink applesauce. It's homemade, so they feel loved, it tastes good, but not too good and its pink which brightens their day.

3 1/2 lbs red apples (about 8), cored and quartered
1 cup apple cider
1 large cinnamon stick
pinch nutmeg
1/4 cup sugar
1 T lemon juice

- In a large saucepan over medium heat add all ingredients and bring to a boil
- Reduce heat, cover and simmer 1 hour, until apples are broken down
- Turn off heat and mix with a potato masher
- Serve warm or cold

Makes approximately 1 quart

Cranberry Sherbet

My neighbor Karen's Thanksgiving tradition is to serve freshly made cranberry sherbet with turkey. Originated by her great grandmother, generations of women in Karen's family have debated over who has the best twist on the recipe: Tart, sweet, crystalline or fluffy. Personal preference depends on how much sugar is used and how long the egg whites are beaten. I'm sticking with Karen's version. I also don't have to tell you, it's a big hit with kids, too…I mean…sherbet *with* dinner? Wow!

2 cups fresh cranberries
2 1/4 cup water
2 cups sugar
1 t gelatin
2 lemons (juice and zest)
2 egg whites

- In a medium saucepan, bring cranberries and water to a boil, then reduce heat to a simmer and cook until soft, 10 minutes
- Drain cranberries, reserving the liquid. Add more water if necessary to equal 2 1/4 cups again. Set aside
- Dissolve gelatin in 2 tablespoons warm water. Let sit 5 minutes
- Place cranberries, gelatin, lemon juice, zest and sugar in a food processor and process to smooth. Place in a medium bowl and freeze for 1 hour
- Meanwhile, in a medium bowl, beat egg whites until stiff peaks form. Fold cranberry mixture into egg whites
- Serve immediately

Serves approximately 10-12

Hot Cider Punch

Every year in early December, my friends Tracy, Betsy, and I go on a locally organized house tour. We spend the morning driving from home to home far grander than our own, peeking in on other people's decorating styles. After the tour, we end up at a little historical house that during the tour is filled with vendors selling holiday gifts and baked goods. We buy one plate of cookies to share and get a cup of free! hot cider. Then we get back in the car and race to school to pick up our kids. The cookies and cider are a perfect reprieve from the day.

1 gallon apple cider
2 cups fresh orange juice
4 T fresh lemon juice
2 t nutmeg
3 t cloves
4 sticks cinnamon
1/2 cup sugar

- In a large pot, combine all ingredients
- Bring to a boil, then reduce to a low simmer (cider can stay simmering until it is finished)
- Serve hot

Serves approximately 20

About the Author

Since she was a young girl growing up in suburban Philadelphia, Amy Currie has been cooking, baking and creating in the kitchen. She was inspired by all that she learned from her grandmother Nanny, before she could even read a recipe. Today she lives with her husband and three children outside of New York City. Entertaining is a big part of Amy's life, but it is the everyday creations in the kitchen that excite her passion for cooking. After a lifetime of cooking for family and friends, she is sharing what she knows in a cookbook about the joys of being a home cook. According to Amy, there is no greater gift than a home cooked meal, and the satisfaction of creating it is deliciously contagious throughout the pages of her memoir.

Index

A

Apple Bread, Chunky, 168
Apple Crisp, 238
Apple Dumplings, 236
Apple Pancake, 169
Apple Pie, Traditional, 235
Apple Sauce, Pink, 256
Artichoke-Proscuitto Gratin, 36
Arugula Salad with Roasted Beets and Goat Cheese, 65
Asparagus Canapés, 12
Asparagus, Grilled, 80
Avocado, Tomato and Cucumber Salad, 73

B

Baba Ghanous, 41
Baby Greens with Warm Goat Cheese, 66
Bacon Toasties, 9
Balsamic Roasted Carrots, 77
Banana Boats, 239
Banana Bread, 167
BB's Ice Box Cookies, 199
Beef Burgundy, 115
Biscotti, Almond Apricot, 203
Black Bean Hummus, 39
Black Bean Soup, Spicy, 60
Black Olive Tapenade, 42, 43
Blondies, Loaded, 205
Blue Cheese and Almond Stuffed Olives, 245
Blueberry Pie, Old Fashioned, 234
Boeuf Bourguignon, 116
Brie with Raspberries, Baked, 26
Brisket, Barbecued, 123
Brisket, Nanny's, 122
Broccoli Puree, 79
Broccoli Soup, 53

Potato Salad, Summer, 92
Potatoes Fabulous, 85
Potatoes, Kristen's, 88
Potatoes, Mini Baked with Sea Salt, 87
Proscuitto and Gruyere Pinwheels, 19

R

Raspberry Cake, Fresh, 227
Red Onion Quiche, 176
Reuben Dip, 32
Rice, Fabulous, 86
Rigatoni, Baked, 98
Roasted Beet and Goat Cheese and Arugula Salad, 65
Roasted Vegetables, 84
Rosemary Scented Mixed Nuts, 243

S

Salmon Mousse with Cucumber Sauce, Cold, 48
Salmon with Cucumber Sauce, Grilled, 149
Salmon with Mustard-Crumb Crust, 152
Salmon, Marinated, Roasted, 151
Salmon, Poached, 150
Sausage Cheese Balls, 11
Sausage Toasties, 10
Sausage, Egg and Cheese Strata, 173
Sautéed Zucchini with Basil, 78
Scallop, Corn and Bacon Burgers, 160
Scallops with Lemon-Mustard Sauce, 157
Sea Bass with Pesto Rub, Roasted, 154
Sesame Noodles with Chicken and Cucumber, 111
Sesame Wonton Crisps, 7
Seven Layer Bars, 214
Shrimp Burgers, 159
Sleigh Ball, 47
Sloppy Joes, 120
Smoked Salmon and Dill Strata, 175
Smoked Salmon Pinwheels, 24
Snickerdoodles, 193

Soft Shell Crabs, Sautéed, 158
Sole with Almonds, Capers and Lemon, Filet of, 156
Sour Cream Chocolate Cake, 219
Spaghetti with Fresh Clams, 108
Spinach and Gruyere Strata, 174
Spinach Au Gratin, 81
Spinach Dip, Fresh, 29
Spinach with Toasted Sesame Seeds, Chopped, 82
Spinach, Wilted, 83
Spinach-Parmesan Dip, Hot, 34
Sticky Buns, 165
Stilton Spread, 45
Stracciatelle with Lemon, 59
Sugar Snap Peas, Roasted, 76
Swedish Pancakes, Thin (Blinis), 170

T

Tamari Sunflower Seeds, 244
Tex Mex Chopped Salad, 72
Toffee Triangles, 208
Tomato Sauce, Summer, 104
Tomato Sauce, Winter, 103
Tomato Tart, 16
Turkey Meatloaf, 140
Turkey Meatloaf Florentine, 141
Turkey Tetrazzini, 145
Turtles, 187

V

Vanilla Thins, 198
Vegetable Cheddar Soup, 52
Vidalia Onion Bread Pudding, 95

W

White Bean and Rosemary Spread, 38
White Bean Soup with Parmesan, 61

Z

Zucchini Pancakes with Chive Crème Fraiche, 14